SECRET SAN FRANCISCO

A GUIDE TO THE WEIRD, WONDERFUL, AND OBSCURE

Ruth Wertzberger Carlson

Reedy Press
PO Box 5131
St. Louis, MO 63139
www.reedypress.com

Library of Congress Control Number: 2018962612
ISBN: 9781681062051

Design by Jill Halpin
Unless otherwise indicated, all photos are courtesy of the author or in the public domain. Photos on pages 89–92, 96–99, 102–105 are courtesy of John Williamson.

Printed in the United States of America
19 20 21 22 23   5 4 3 2 1

DEDICATION

This book is dedicated to my late husband, Richard Carlson.

CONTENTS

ACKNOWLEDGMENTS

I feel so lucky to call this city my home. Growing up in Dubuque, Iowa, nicknamed little San Francisco thanks to its hills overlooking the water (the Mississippi river) and its lone cable car, I dreamed of living in San Francisco, and now I wrote a book about my beloved city.

So many people helped me with this book I can't name them all, but must give a shout out to John Williamson who contributed numerous photos, Joe Butler, John Law, Patrick Rylee, Laurie Armstrong and her team at sftravel.com, Molly Blaisdell who lent me her mother's historic archives, Bernadette Festa and Elizabeth Coieman who supported me every step of the way, Janet and Mike Hilby who helped me scout locations, my researcher Jillian Wertzberger and my nine siblings and cousins who pre-ordered copies of my first book. I love this city so much; I hope the locals will forgive me when they discover I inevitably made a mistake.

INTRODUCTION

Why are the streets of San Francisco paved with old gravestones? Who built a hidden labyrinth on a cliff at Land's End? What is a huge fiberglass dog's head doing in the middle of Sloat Boulevard? These are just a few of the tantalizing questions answered in *Secret San Francisco: a Guide to the Weird, Wonderful, and Obscure*.

More than twenty-five million people visit the city each year, but most never get beyond Pier 29, the Golden Gate Bridge, and Alcatraz. This guidebook is for the intrepid traveler eager to discover the city's surprises and for locals thrilled to learn something new about their beloved city.

For a relatively small city (800,000 residents) and only forty-seven square miles, San Francisco has an amazing array of attractions. Each neighborhood holds surprises most residents try to keep for themselves. From the Avenues to Little Italy and all along the waterfront, there are hidden treasures if you just know where to look.

To uncover the city's mysteries, I called old friends, made many new ones, and visited places that weren't on Google Maps. I interviewed bartenders, archivists, artists, leaders of secret societies, and most of all the quirky characters who keep San Francisco weird.

1 Al's Attire

What are those eccentric outfits on display in North Beach?

Victorian-era leather boots, 1950s-style dresses, and military jackets in the windows of Al's Attire cause people to do a double take, which is just what Al Ribaya wants them to do. Al's Attire is a made-to-order clothing store. "We're the only place in the city that still makes custom apparel from head to toe," says Al. Anything you can imagine he can create: hats, suits, coats, dresses, and shoes for adults and children. "Sometimes I have to explain to customers that their concept will not work. I had to tell a woman that if I made her shoes they would be the ugliest ever."

Couture created specifically to fit one person's measurements is a dying art. "People don't understand the sourcing, you can't just go to Heels R Us," says Al. He even has a team that embroiders, makes buttonholes, and dyes fabrics. Movie stars frequent his shop and he's catching on with young techies. "Some of them get the concept but they don't always like coming back for fittings," he says.

Self-taught, Al says he became a tailor to get a girl. "It didn't work," he laughs, "but I'm still working." He's an artist, but instead of watercolors or clay, his medium is lux fabrics he sources from around the world. When you walk into the store you'll often see him expertly and gracefully cutting fabric for a dress or placing leather around a shoe form. Even the clothing labels for Al's Attire are a work of art—so distinctive you're tempted to wear the clothes inside out.

His décor, with hatboxes and vintage signs, is as interesting as the fashion.

If you're lucky you might see Al creating couture garments.

HABERDASHERY HEAVEN

WHAT Al's Attire

WHERE 1300 Grant St.

COST Free to browse but be careful: the selection is tempting.

PRO TIP If a tiny detail is wrong in a consignment, Al sells it in the store at a discount.

2 A BOOK CLUB OPRAH WOULD LOVE

Where can bibliophiles go in San Francisco?

When your arms are aching from carrying heavy shopping bags, your credit cards are screaming for mercy, and your brain demands culture, you can find relief at a secret haven downtown.

Entering the paneled walls of the Book Club of California, you'll wish you splurged and purchased that fancy hat; these rooms transport visitors to another era. Sinking into a red leather chair near the fireplace, you'll gaze upon bookshelves lined with historical manuscripts. It resembles a private men's club, but looks are deceiving; this is a non-profit organization, free, and open to the public.

Anxious to show the world how sophisticated San Francisco had become, local dignitaries formed The Book Club of California in 1912 and planned a rare book display at the World's Fair. For some reason their exhibition never happened but the Book Club remained. Women were even allowed to join, including Phoebe Hearst, mother of William Randolph Hearst.

More than a reading room, the Book Club is dedicated to all aspects of fine printing, including typography, paper quality, binding, and illustration. It has the only letterpress journal in

---

The Holiday Card Exhibit is the most popular event of the year.

A private club anyone can enjoy.

the country still in existence and it also publishes limited edition books on California history and literature. Among the recent exhibits and events were *Rock 'N' Roll Billboards of the Sunset Strip* and a lecture by a cartoon illustrator. "If you love books and reading and history, you'll love something about The Book Club," says Executive Director Kevin Kiosk.

BOOK IT

WHAT The Book Club of California

WHERE 312 Sutter St.

COST Free for drop-ins, various prices for membership.

PRO TIP On the opening night of an exhibit, the Book Club sponsors receptions at their bar.

3 EMPEROR WITH NO CLOTHES

When did a royal rule San Francisco?

Police saluted him, he printed his own currency, and the military gave him uniforms.

San Francisco's Emperor Norton wasn't born into royalty. Joshua Norton moved here in 1849 and quickly became successful. When he tried to corner the rice market he lost his fortune and it appears his mind. After leaving the city in disgrace he returned a few years later wearing an ostrich-plumed hat, a navy coat with epaulets, and a saber. He marched into the offices of the Call Bulletin announcing that he was Emperor of the United States and the indulgent newspaper printed his edict, beginning two decades of his rule.

San Francisco was in a recession and Norton was a welcome distraction according to Joseph Amster, who leads Emperor Norton's Fantastic San Francisco Time Machine tour. "Many scholars believe the king in *Huckleberry Finn* is based on him," says Amster.

Restaurants let him eat for free, he spent his evenings at the opera and ballet, the Masons paid for his lodging, and the military gave him new uniforms. Emperor Norton created his own currency and sold it out to people in Portsmouth Square, charging anywhere from fifty cents to ten dollars.

Norton was eccentric but also a visionary. He decreed the city should build a bridge to Oakland sixty years before the

---

There are ongoing efforts to rename the Bay Bridge the Emperor Norton Bridge.

Be sure to bow if you see the Emperor.

AN ECCENTRIC RULER

WHAT Emperor Norton's Fantastic Time Machine tours

WHERE Ferry Building

COST $30.00 adults, $15.00 children

PRO TIP Check Goldstar before buying tickets for the tour; they're often half off.

Bay Bridge was constructed. He was in favor of women's rights, against racial injustice, dreamed up the League of Nations, and banned the city nickname "Frisco"—still a popular sentiment with most locals.

When he died, thousands of mourners showed up for his funeral, and Amster claims that as his coffin was lowered there was a total eclipse of the sun.

4 HOTEL WITH A HEART

What do the Beatles, Barbra Streisand, and Dan Quayle have in common?

Compared with the Palace Hotel, Mark Hopkins, and St. Francis, the Hilton Union Square is the new kid on the block, but it still has plenty of history.

Built in 1964, it's the largest hotel west of the Mississippi (with the exception of gambling hotels) and home to the city's third-highest bridge, the sky bridge on the sixteenth floor.

The Beatles stayed here before they performed at Candlestick Park, their final concert, and one enterprising employee took their sheets and towels, ripped them up, and sold scraps to screaming fans outside the hotel.

It's where Dan Quayle made his infamous remarks about Murphy Brown in 1992. Speaking to the Commonwealth Club, the vice president said the TV character Murphy Brown, played by Candice Bergen, was wrong in choosing to be a single mother. When she won an Emmy, she thanked Quayle and hasn't forgotten him. In the rebooted sitcom, Murphy Brown made a dig at Quayle in the first episode.

The Hilton was the Bristol Hotel in the movie *What's Up Doc*? with several key scenes filmed here including Barbra Streisand and Ryan O'Neill singing "As Time Goes By" in the Cityscape Lounge.

The Hilton Union Square provides up to three thousand pounds of compost daily, which is distributed to farms in Northern California.

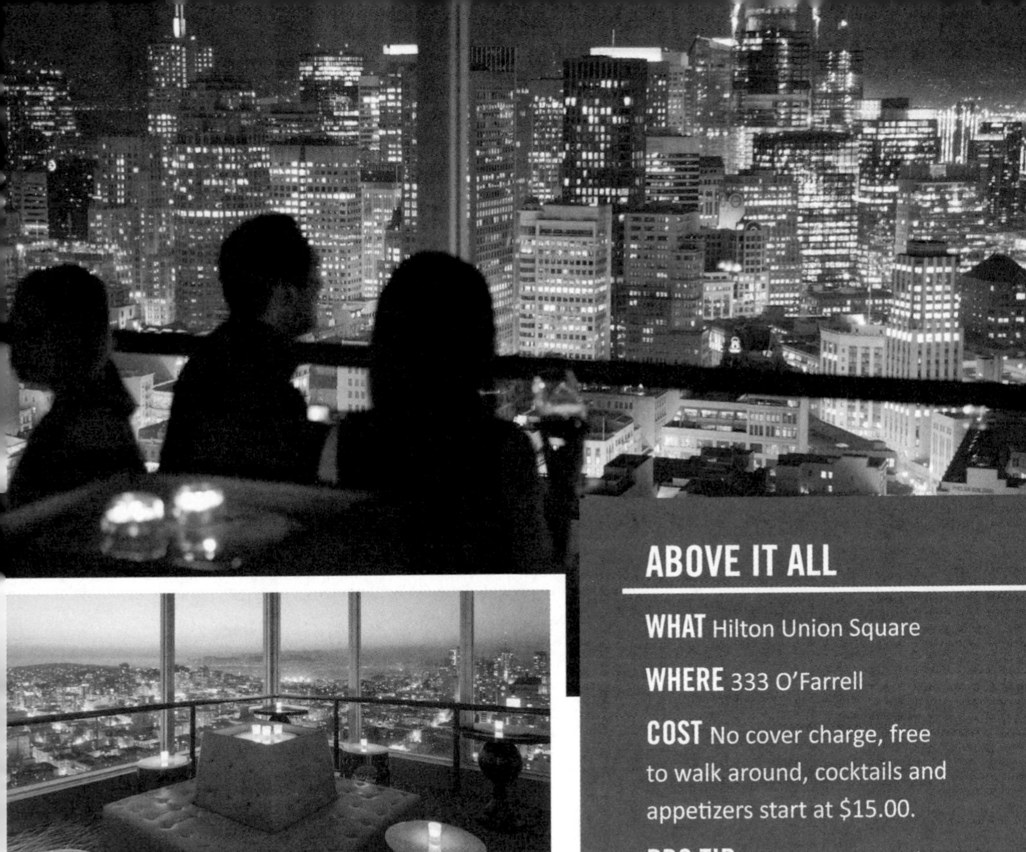

The Hilton also has an award-winning restaurant, The Urban Tavern.

ABOVE IT ALL

WHAT Hilton Union Square

WHERE 333 O'Farrell

COST No cover charge, free to walk around, cocktails and appetizers start at $15.00.

PRO TIP Cityscape located on the 46th floor of the Hilton Union Square is considered the highest bar in San Francisco with unobstructed panoramic views.

The hotel continues to make news today as one of the largest contributors to the Tenderloin, an economically depressed neighborhood near Union Square. They hired a Community Projects Manager, Jo Licata, who says, "As the largest employer in the area we had to show the neighbors a human face to the brick and mortar of our entity."

5 FLOAT IN NORTH BEACH

What's one of the best free events of the year?

Ask a San Franciscan where they live and they won't say the city: they'll proudly name their neighborhood instead. In the mere forty-nine miles that make up San Francisco you can find: Chinatown, Japantown, a large Hispanic population in the Mission, the legacy of African American jazz clubs in the Fillmore, and Little Italy in North Beach.

North Beach hosts the city's oldest civic event and the nation's oldest Italian American Heritage Parade dating back to 1868. It starts at Fisherman's Wharf and ends in North Beach.

Restaurants place their tables on the sidewalk so diners have a front row seat for marching bands, floats, dancers, and the Blue Angels flying over Coit Tower. (The parade takes place each October during Fleet Week).

Before the parade hundreds of people outfitted in red and green—the Italian flag colors—admire the Ferraris on display in Washington Square Park while sipping espressos and sampling cannoli. Italians take great pride in their contributions to San Francisco. Notable Italian Americans from San

SHOWING THEIR COLORS

WHAT Italian American Heritage Parade

WHERE North Beach

COST Free

PRO TIP Make a restaurant reservation so you have guaranteed front row seats.

Alcatraz Island hosts two Indigenous Peoples' Day events annually. In 1969 Native Americans, including actor Benjamin Bratt, occupied Alcatraz for nineteen months to protest federal policies.

Locals call this the best event of the year. Bernadette Festa dances in the parade each year with other members of Le Donne d'Italia.

Francisco include Joe DiMaggio, A. P. Giannini, whose small Bank of Italy became Bank of America, and Domenico Ghiradelli's contribution to our waistlines, and poet Lawrence Ferlinghetti, founder of the City Lights Bookstore in the 1950s that became a haven for "beat" writers.

In 2018 the San Francisco Board of Supervisors voted to change the name of Columbus Day to Indigenous Peoples' Day, which was not popular with either the Italian American community or the local Ohlone Indian tribe, according to the *San Francisco Chronicle*. A compromise was struck with the help of the Ohlones, and Columbus Day in San Francisco was renamed Italian American Heritage Day.

6 PEEPHOLE CINEMA

A Hole in the Wall

Only a tiny sign with an eyeball on it dangling on a red wall in an alleyway lets you know you've arrived at the Peephole Cinema. It plays continuous short silent films for anyone willing to look into this hole in the wall.

"There's a tradition of graffiti art in the Mission District and I like to think of this as film graffiti," says the creator, Laurie O'Brien. The idea came from film festivals. "I looked around the room and everyone was an animator, so I devised a way to show their films to a wider audience," she says. The films, which she curates, are constantly rotating. Movie titles appear on a small sign.

ANIMATED ART

WHAT Peephole Cinema

WHERE 280 Orange Alley-behind Valencia and 26th St.

COST Free

PRO TIP Any alleyway can be dangerous at night, so it's best to go during daylight hours.

Peephole cinemas, such as the Kinetoscope Parlor, have always interested her. Invented by Thomas Edison, the Kinetoscope passes a strip of film quickly between a lens and an electric light bulb while the viewer peers through a dime-sized hole. One of the first Kinetoscopes was installed on Market Street in the 1890s.

"In the beginning everyone watched films individually in a box. That was replaced by movie theaters, and now we're back to individual films on our computers," observes O'Brien. Ironically, she notes that technology has made this antique form of watching films more accessible due to the ease of downloading films.

O'Brien's miniature cinema has spread to Los Angeles and Brooklyn. Recently, the San Francisco International Airport

After the peephole cinema check out The San Francisco Film Festival, the longest running film festival in the United States.

commissioned her to create an original film for a peephole cinema installation.

O'Brien says this is a labor of love and "as long as I'm alive, peephole cinema will continue 24-7."

You can see another early motion picture device, the Mutoscope, at the Musée Mécanique along Fisherman's Wharf.

7 HISTORIC WINS

What team scores home runs with the community?

Fans know the stats for all the players, but the Giants' legacy goes beyond winning the World Series. Here are a few other ways they've been number one:

The team was the first major league team to hire a female public address announcer, Sherry Davis. Renel Brooks-Moon, the current announcer, is the longest running African American female announcer for MLB and only the second African American woman ever in this position. As the first female public address announcer for a World Series, she's in the Baseball Hall of Fame. Brooks-Moon has been with the team since Oracle Park was built and claims that workers placed some items to be saved for prosperity inside the field's huge Giant Glove—but she's sworn to secrecy.

Oracle is the only ballpark where players can hit homeruns that might land in water . . . nicknamed "a splash hit." On game days, the Willie McCovey Cove is very popular with fans who hang out in kayaks and sailboats, hoping to catch balls.

The ballpark is on a small parcel of land—just thirteen acres. As a result, Oracle has one of the shortest right fields in baseball and one of the deepest center fields.

If you're confused about the name Oracle Park, it's understandable. After twenty years, the AT&T contract ended and Oracle took over the naming rights.

The Giants transformed the neglected waterfront.

A GIGANTIC INFLUENCE

WHAT Oracle Park Tour

WHERE Oracle Park

COST Prices listed on website.

PRO TIP Fans can watch games for free by peeking through the portholes located in the right field wall off the Portwalk along McCovey Cove.

Even one of the entrances to the park is unique. Lefty O'Doul Bridge is a working drawbridge that carried streetcars and trains in 1933. Named after Francis Joseph "Lefty" O'Doul, one of San Francisco's most popular ballplayers, the bridge was designed by Joseph Strauss, also responsible for the Golden Gate Bridge.

More than twenty years ago the Giants were the first MLB team to use senior citizens as ball boys and ball girls and broadcasters changed their name to ball dudes and ball dudettes. Their grandkids are allowed to run the bases every Sunday after a day game.

When the Giants win, they're the only team to play the song "I Left my Heart in San Francisco."

8 CAMERA OBSCURA

What was Leonardo da Vinci's contribution to San Francisco?

Before Instagram, drones, and smartphones, San Franciscans visited the Giant Camera to see panoramic views of Ocean Beach.

Camera Obscura uses a Leonardo da Vinci invention to show real-time images in a dark room. (*Obscura* means "dark" in Latin). A pinhole opening reflects an external object or scene upside down onto a flat surface and a lens reverts the image so it appears right-side up. This simple technique was an important discovery for photography.

The Giant Camera building is the last remaining structure from Playland at the Beach, an amusement park which operated along the Great Highway from 1928 to 1972. When Playland closed, the Giant Camera was slated to be destroyed until it was saved by public outcry. Now it's protected as a building on the National Register of Historic Places.

BEST VIEWS OF OCEAN BEACH

WHAT Giant Camera

WHERE Behind the Cliff House, 1090 Point Lobos Ave.

COST $3.00

PRO TIP The best time to visit is just before sunset. Call ahead to confirm they're open, since the hours can be erratic.

Don't miss the historic holograms lining the walls.

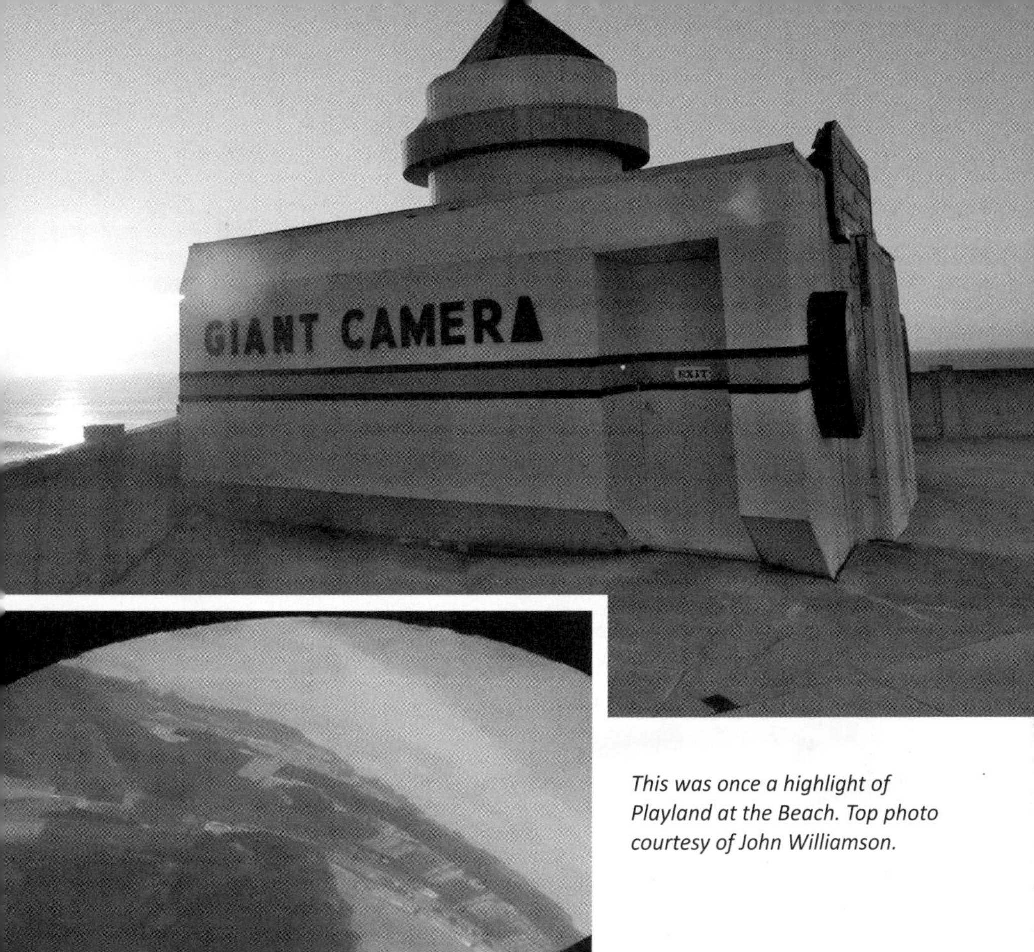

This was once a highlight of Playland at the Beach. Top photo courtesy of John Williamson.

9 PHANTOM FLEET

Did you ever wonder what's under the sidewalk?

How fitting that the Financial District, home to high-tech giants and formerly the site of the Pacific Stock Exchange, is built over ships abandoned during the Gold Rush.

In 1848 the world descended on the sleepy town of San Francisco. As soon as vessels reached the harbor, sailors, and even some officers, headed for the Mother Lode, seduced by tales of instant riches, and the boats were left to rot.

Instead of finding the empty ships a nuisance the city saw opportunities. With the exploding population and land in short supply, developers solved the problem by covering ships with landfill. If you owned your boat you could claim the land underneath it, leading some skippers to purposefully sink their ships.

Workers discovered one of those boats in the 1990s while digging a tunnel to extend the N-Judah streetcar line. Today passengers going south of market travel through the Rome ship's hull without even realizing it. Back in 2001, the *General Harrison* was uncovered during construction downtown. It became the foundation (again) of an eleven-story building.

With the help of archeologists, the San Francisco Maritime Museum has created a new map of these buried ships, the first one since the 1960s. One of their discoveries was a shipyard at Rincon Point, where boats were dismantled for their bronze, brass, and wood, valuable commodities in those days.

If you hike along Lands End Trail, you can see three ships that crashed and were never removed.

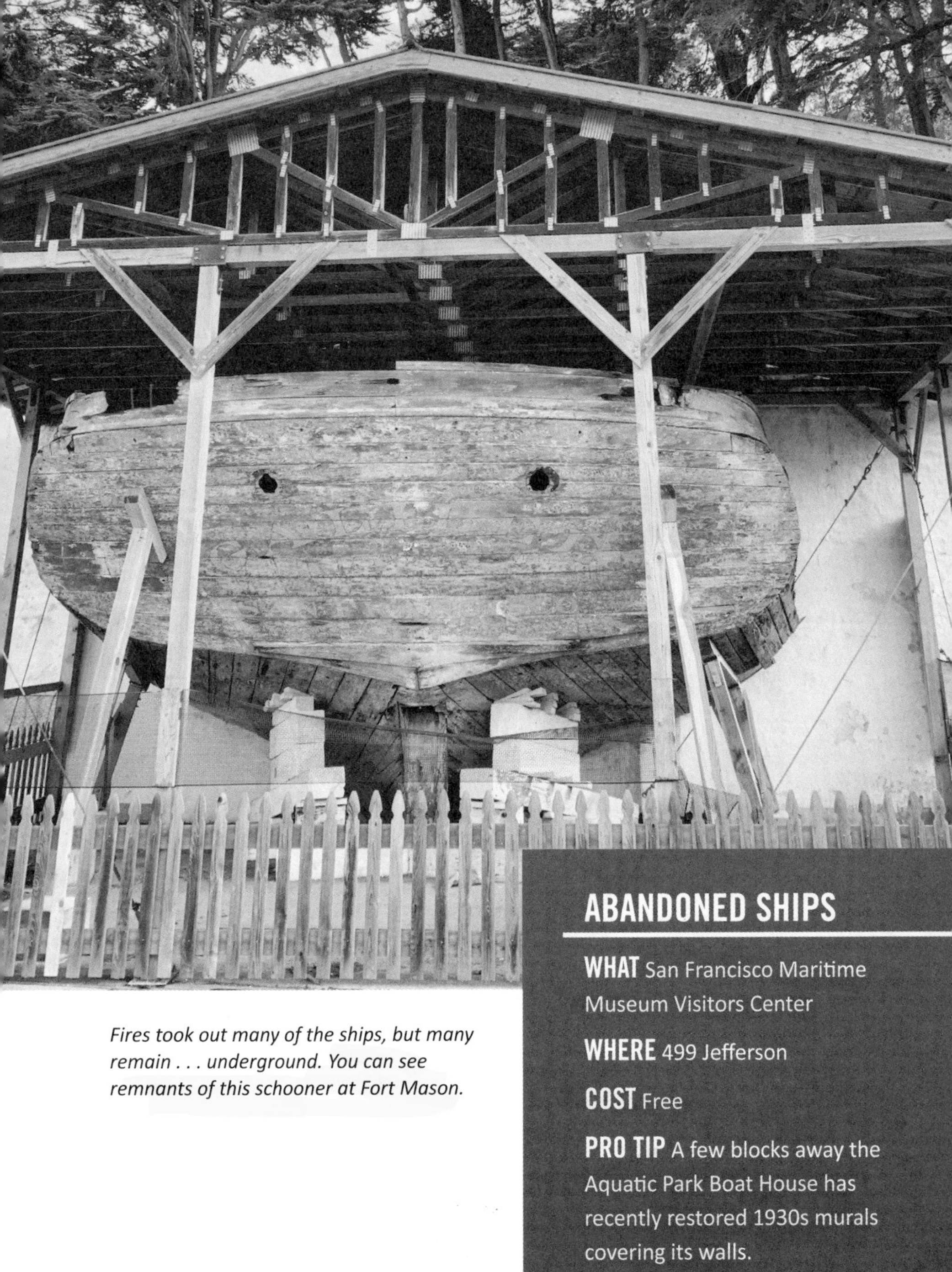

Fires took out many of the ships, but many remain . . . underground. You can see remnants of this schooner at Fort Mason.

ABANDONED SHIPS

WHAT San Francisco Maritime Museum Visitors Center

WHERE 499 Jefferson

COST Free

PRO TIP A few blocks away the Aquatic Park Boat House has recently restored 1930s murals covering its walls.

10 BURNING MAN

How did thousands of people decide to gather in the middle of nowhere each year?

Everyone's heard about the annual wild rave party in the desert called "Burning Man" where artists gather to create gigantic sculptures. But did you know it started in San Francisco in the 80s with a handful of friends torching a ten-foot tall figure out of wood at Baker Beach?

San Franciscan John Law was there in the early days along with his friends in the Cacophony Society, an underground group of pranksters and performance artists known for staging secret elaborate clandestine events in tunnels, bridges, sewers, and abandoned buildings. Their motto was "Live each day as though it were your last."

Each year the bonfire gathering grew in size until 1990 when the Park Police shut it down. Law and another Cacophony member, Kevin Evans, suggested moving the event to Black Rock Desert. The plan was to create a temporary city of art in the desolate desert, bringing all their supplies with them. "We all donated our expertise, I did neon so I handled that," says Law.

About seventy people made it to the first Burning Man in the desert, which was free. The next year it doubled in size, and in 2018 seventy thousand attended and paid $425.00 for a ticket that was hard to come by.

Locals joke that they encouraged Burning Man to move to the desert so they could find parking during the tourist season.

It started out as a simple party on Baker Beach. Photo courtesy of John Law.

Burning Man is its own city with its own laws and rules: bring in your own supplies and beg, borrow, or create whatever else you need. Critics say the event has changed from an informal collaboration of artists to a corporate retreat. Many tech CEOs return to Burning Man annually because they say it makes them more creative and better at their jobs.

A SAN FRANCISCO CULTURAL CONTRIBUTION

WHAT The origins of Burning Man

WHERE Baker Beach

COST Free if you visit the original site, Baker Beach.

PRO TIP The Cacophony Society no longer exists but artists are still holding innovative events all over the city. Johnwlaw.com lists many of them.

11 FISHY TALE

Who invented Cioppino?

The origins of this tomato-based seafood stew are as hazy as the fog that permeates San Francisco. Even the name is in question. Some say it comes from the Genoese word "little soup," but the more appealing story is that in the late 1800s North Beach fishermen who returned to the wharf empty-handed passed around a pot to their friends and said "chip in," which turned into cioppino.

One thing everyone agrees on is that this seafood stew is delicious. A tomato base with Dungeness crab, shrimp, clams, flaky fish, onions, and garlic, it's as connected to the city as the wharf. After the quake in 1906 a cookbook was released to raise money for the refugees, and one of the recipes was a dish called cioppino.

Alioto's is credited with being the first restaurant to serve the stew. Nunzio Alioto opened a stall selling lunch to fishermen in 1925, and when he died his widow Rose became the first woman to work on the wharf. She opened Alioto's restaurant, where cioppino was always on the menu.

SAN FRANCISCO'S SEAFOOD STEW

WHAT Cioppino

WHERE Restaurants serving fresh fish

COST Varies

PRO TIP Scoma's is one of the few places in the city where you can get valet parking for free.

One of the few remaining wooden sidewalks in the city is outside Scoma's.

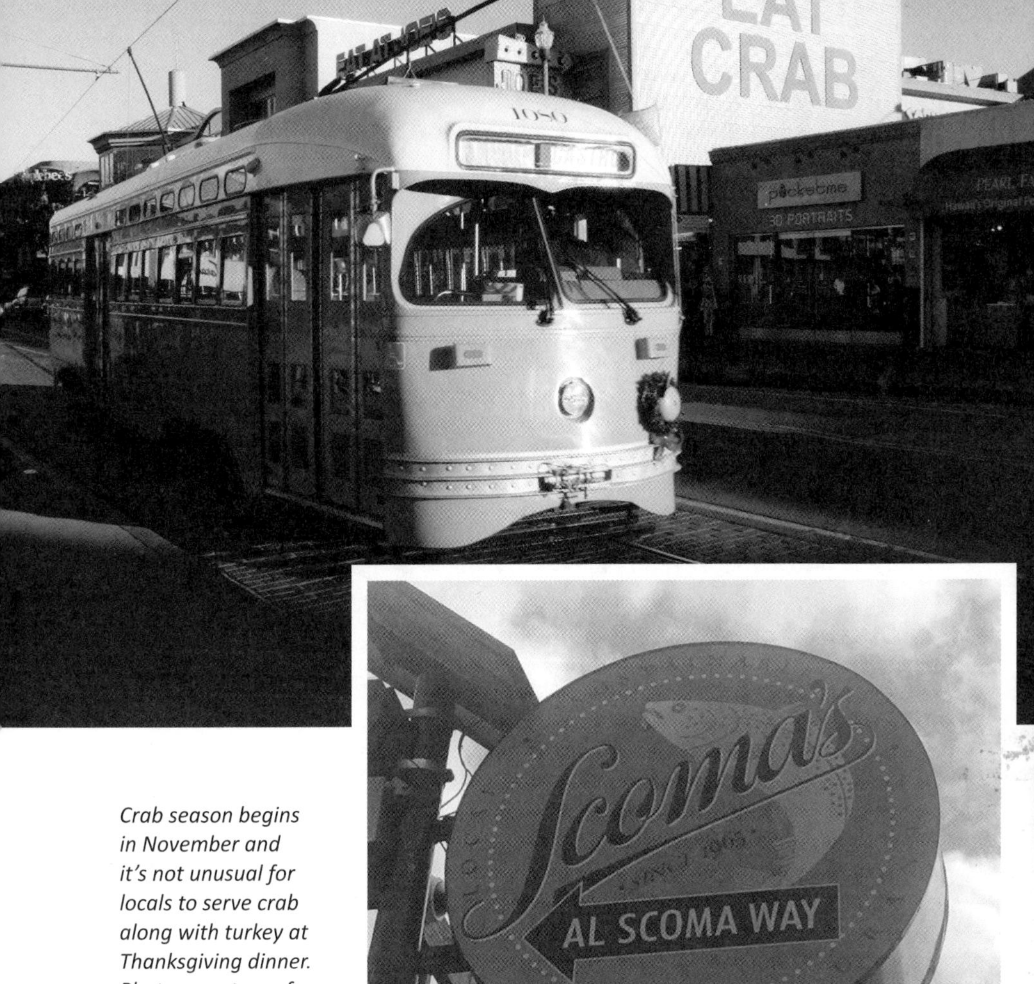

Crab season begins in November and it's not unusual for locals to serve crab along with turkey at Thanksgiving dinner. Photos courtesy of John Williamson.

Just down the block, Scoma's, another family-owned business, serves lazy man's cioppino, so named because the crab is already cracked for you. Scoma's is the only restaurant in San Francisco with a fish receiving station. Small fishing boats deliver their fresh catch directly to the station where they are prepped for dinner. Scoma's calls it "pier to plate."

12 COSTLY CABLE CARS

Who saved the cable cars?

It's hard to imagine New York City without the Empire State Building, Paris without the Eiffel Tower, or San Francisco without cable cars . . . and yet it almost happened . . . twice. The cost of keeping this moving national monument running has always been an issue.

In 1947 Mayor Roger Lapham wanted to replace the "old-fashioned" cable cars with diesel buses, and he was making great headway until Friedel Klussmann put on the brakes. She started a campaign with the motto "There'll always be cable cars in San Francisco." It got national attention; *Life* magazine did a story, and celebrities—including Eleanor Roosevelt—voiced their support.

In the early 1980s the cable cars were in danger again. Dilapidated and accident prone, the whole system needed a complete overhaul but that meant removing the cars from the streets for two years and spending $60 million. Taxpayers protested and one contingent wanted the cable cars eliminated.

Mayor Dianne Feinstein began a campaign to save them. She

THERE'LL ALWAYS BE CABLE CARS IN SAN FRANCISCO

WHAT Cable Car Museum

WHERE 1201 Mason St.

COST Free

PRO TIP Skip the long lines at Powell St. and Ghirardelli Square and grab a ride on the California Cable Car line, always the least crowded.

When she was just a teenager, Maya Angelou became the first African American female cable car conductor.

Get a clipper card to save money on the costly cable cars. Photos courtesy of John Williamson.

had secured the next Democratic Convention for San Francisco and wanted to make a good impression. Her most famous endorser was Mick Jagger who was in town for a concert. He posed on an electric cable car for reporters and said, “Once they’re gone you can’t get them back.”

Mick did the trick: the money was raised and Feinstein was able to save the cable cars. The first day the refurbished cars were on the street she wanted Tony Bennett aboard singing his valentine to San Francisco—but that’s another story!

13 MEOW FOR THE MASSES

Who has purrfect tea service?

Tea parties sound rather upper crust but the hosts of this one are exceedingly casual. Don't be surprised if they jump in your lap, pounce on the furniture, or ignore you all together. They're sanctuary cats who invite people over for green tea—it was only a matter of time before the rock stars of Facebook ruled our society.

While visiting Japan the founders came across a cat café and decided to open one in SF. The owners of KitTea Cat Café claim it's the first established cat café in the United States.

If you google "cats and health," you'll get all kinds of stories claiming that cats can reduce stress, help you sleep better, and improve your mood. Advocats (get it?) say the purr vibration gives you a feeling like oxytocin and will even heal bones! Whether there is scientific evidence for these claims or not, office workers swear that escaping from their cubicles to cuddle cats improves their mood.

CAT THERAPY

WHAT Tea with cats

WHERE 96 Gough St.

COST $25 for an hour on weekends

PRO TIP The small gift shop has some low-cost items for that cat-crazed person in your life . . . and you know you have at least one.

Love cats but you're allergic? You can still watch their antics behind a glass window in the café.

Jillian Wertzberger swears by the calming effects of cats.

It's a very simple concept: drink tea and pet cats for an hour—and people pay money for this? Well, it is San Francisco. The sterile room has a cat wheel, toys, and mazes, but the cats seem happiest purring in a human's lap. They're all rescue cats, but many are resident kitties. The ones with collars are available for adoption. You're not allowed to pick them up, which would allow the cats to feel comfortable approaching you, according to the "cat wrangler," the staff member who makes sure you don't let the cats out the door.

In addition to tea you can sign up for game night with kitties, including the Crazy Cat Lady game, Mewie (movie) Night, Caturday Morning Cartoons (where cat jammies are optional), or you can reach purrvana at Yoga with Cats.

14 IT'S A WONDERFUL LIFE

Who was the inspiration for George Bailey?

The stories about A. P. Giannini (the founder of Bank of America) are endless. He financed the movie Snow White during the depression, he created bank branching, and he pulled off a heist from his own bank. People debate details about his life but everyone agrees he never forgot his working class roots.

Giannini was raised on Telegraph Hill when it was a middle-class neighborhood. His neighbor was Tom Crowley and their friendship would save Bank of Italy (later named Bank of America) according to Crowley's nephew, Tom Escher.

This is where the story gets complicated. The Bank of America archivist says that after the 1906 quake Giannini hid the bank's money in a vegetable cart and transported it across the Bay but the Escher family version is more intriguing. After the 1906 quake Giannini was nervous the city could burn down, and asked Crowley, who had a shipping business, to hide the bank's money in milk cans and ship it across the Bay. When the boat arrived in Berkeley no was there to meet it—so the skipper—believing it was just milk—left the cans on the dock. The next day, Giannini located the correct dock and the milk cans, filled with millions of dollars, were still sitting there.

After the citywide fires were extinguished, Giannini placed a plank on two barrels along the waterfront and opened a

---

Immediately following the quake, Giannini was one of the few banks with money. Because of the fires bank owners were unable to open their vaults for days—the heat would ignite the cash.

Some events held at the private Wingtip club are open to the public, such as the Kentucky Derby Party.

temporary bank. He loaned the money (primarily to working-class Italian Americans he knew by name) with just a handshake. Legend has it they all paid him back.

Because of this story, and Giannini's friendship with Frank Capra, many say the George Bailey character in *It's a Wonderful Life* was loosely based on Giannini.

IT'S A WONDERFUL LIFE

WHAT The former Bank of Italy, a national historic landmark building, now Wingtip, a private club

WHERE 550 Montgomery

COST Anyone can enter the shops and barbershops downstairs. The upper floors are a private club.

PRO TIP Be sure to visit the safe, which is now a cigar humidor.

15 FLYING BOATS

What happened to Treasure Island Airport?

Like a mirage, it appeared before San Francisco, built of rocks and mud and perhaps some gold from the Bay. Treasure Island, created for the 1939 Golden Gate International Exposition, was slated to become an airport for Pan Am's Clipper Ships—planes that landed on water, or "flying boats."

Pan Am had just made the first transpacific flight in history, and city fathers anticipated a big demand for international travel. San Francisco got as far as building an Art Moderne terminal, lined with a massive mural depicting naval history, when World War II changed everything.

The military commandeered the island and when the war was over, flying had changed forever, and clipper ships were passé. In exchange for keeping the island, the military offered the city vacant land on the peninsula, now called San Francisco International Airport, code name SFO.

TREASURE ISLAND MUSEUM

WHAT The airport that never took off

WHERE 1 Avenue of the Palms, Treasure Island

COST Free

PRO TIP The best way to see the island is on two wheels. Visit the Trans Bay Bike Shop, started by a woman who was once homeless.

See what it was like in the glamorous days of flying: visit the Oakland Airport Aircraft Museum, which houses the flying boat owned by Howard Hughes.

Treasure Island has some of the best views of San Francisco. Photos courtesy of John Williamson.

In 1996 the military left Treasure Island and developers lined up to build condos and hotels until they hit a snafu: some of the land was thought to be contaminated by nuclear weapons tested on boats in the Pacific. Environmental cleanup is under way, but in the meantime, Treasure Island's aircraft hangars are used as sound stages for movies like *Indiana Jones and the Last Crusade*. A massive flea market takes place on weekends in the warmer months and a brewery and some wineries have sprouted along the waterfront.

16 LAWN BOWLING

What ancient game is a modern escape?

Golden Gate Park is home to the oldest lawn bowling club in the nation and they have John McLaren to thank. A Scotsman, he designed Golden Gate Park and believed a proper park must have lawns for bowling. In 1901 he was a founding member of the San Francisco Scottish Bowling Club that later changed its name to the San Francisco Bowling Club. Another founding member was San Francisco mayor "Sunny Jim" Rolph, who became governor of California.

Similar to bocce ball, the object of the game is rolling a biased ball, called a "bowl," close to the jack, a small white ball. "It's kind of amazing that you can train your body to roll this oblong and asymmetrical object with accuracy," says member Daniel Gorelick, who competes in tournaments.

Gorelick explains, "The game is kind of addicting: once you make a good shot you want to do it again." He thinks it usually takes about three lessons to get the hang of the nuances, strategy, and rules of the game. Some say bocce is like checkers and lawn bowling is like chess. Luckily the club offers free lessons Wednesdays and Saturdays at noon. "Bowls is a great equalizer," says Club President John Grimes. "Men and women play equally well."

Golden Gate Park is 20 percent larger than New York's Central Park.

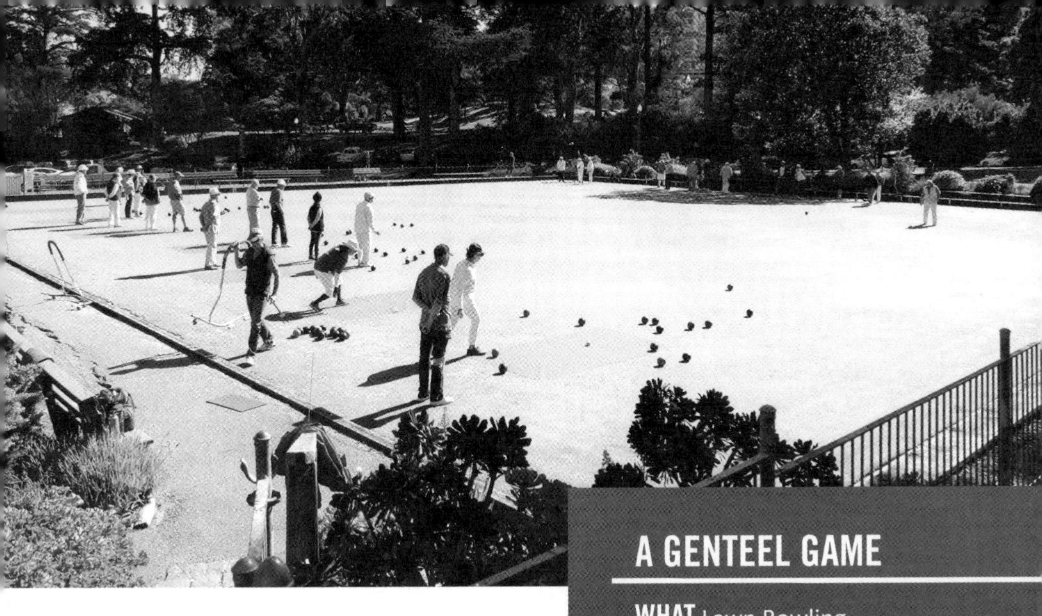

Golden Gate Park also has a horseshoe club.

A GENTEEL GAME

WHAT Lawn Bowling

WHERE Golden Gate Park next to Sharon Meadow.

COST Free lessons, $130 annually for membership.

PRO TIP Only flat-soled shoes are allowed on the green.

Gardeners keep the three manicured bowling courts—which are ADA compliant—lush with recycled water. "The greens are so majestic and regal, you feel like you're on a giant putting green," says Gorelick.

Many members find lawn bowling a great way to unwind with friends after work. There's a social gathering the second Tuesday of each month in the Edwardian-style clubhouse filled with century-old memorabilia. When members dress in all white attire, customary for tournaments, you're transported back to 1914 when the landmark building was constructed. In 2019 the Club is hosting the National Championship.

17 ESCAPE FROM THE CONCRETE

What is a POPOS?

There's a softer side to the financial district's imposing high-rises. Secret gardens, atriums, rooftop terraces, and patios are waiting for you to visit. POPOS—privately owned public open spaces—are open to everyone.

It's a deal the city made with developers in 1985. The Downtown Plan requires private skyscrapers to create spaces, often with outdoor art, that the public can use.

Signage can be minimal: look for a picture of a tree with the words "Public Open Space," but if you can't find it, don't let that stop you. SFplanning.org and Spur.org have maps of all sixty-eight spaces.

Here are a few that stand out:

Redwood Forest: Below the Transamerica Pyramid—the city's tallest building before Salesforce—stands a redwood forest with eighty mature trees uprooted from the Santa Cruz mountains. Sitting among these ancient trees that soften the sound of sirens, buses, and cellphone jabber, it's hard to believe you're surrounded by steel-and-glass towers. In a

REAL ESTATE FOR THE MASSES

WHAT Public parks in private buildings

WHERE Anywhere there is a skyscraper: downtown, Financial District, and South of Market.

COST Free

PRO TIP POPOS are usually only open during business hours.

San Francisco, New York, and Seattle are among the few cities that require POPOS.

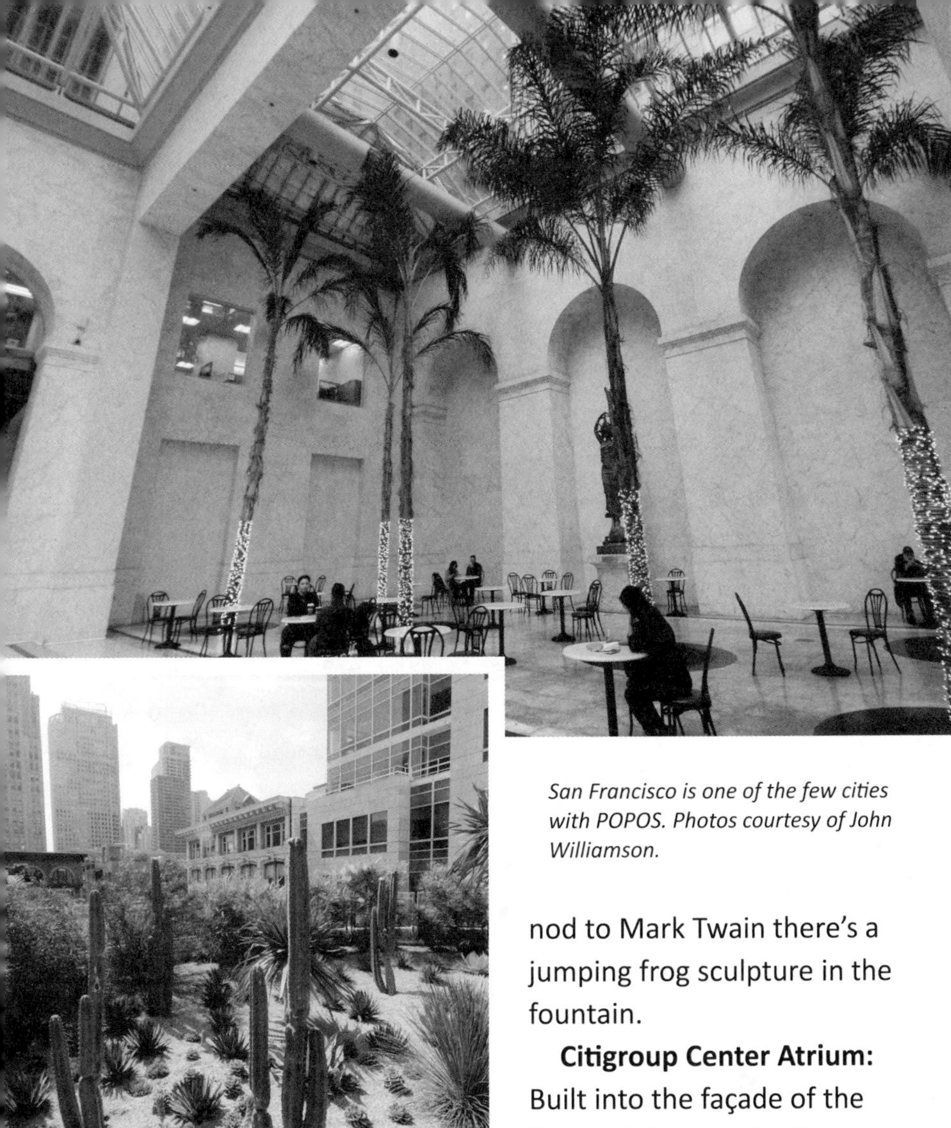

San Francisco is one of the few cities with POPOS. Photos courtesy of John Williamson.

nod to Mark Twain there's a jumping frog sculpture in the fountain.

Citigroup Center Atrium: Built into the façade of the former 1912 London Paris Bank building is a sun-filled plaza with queen palm trees, a marble floor, fountain and a replica of the Star Maiden statue from the Pan Pacific Exposition.

Sansome Roof Garden: An obelisk sundial is at the center of this fifteen-story-high oasis. The olive trees shade the benches and tables with a view of the Bay, the Transamerica Pyramid and the three twelve-foot-high statues in robes named *Corporate Goddesses*.

18 STAIRWAYS TO HEAVEN

How do you see the real San Francisco?

San Francisco is often called the most European city in America and like Europeans, we love to walk, especially on hidden, romantic, steep stairways that take us to places you can't see in a car or a bus. There are over six hundred stairways in the city: stairways lined with mosaic tile, stairways of sand, stairways leading to landmarks, and all with amazing views.

Why so many stairs in this city that covers only forty-nine square miles? When the city was formed, horses were unable to pull carriages up the steepest hills so they built stairways for pedestrians.

Here are a few that stand out:

16th Avenue and Moraga: This mosaic tile stairway with the theme "Flowing Sea to Stars" was a labor of love by the neighbors.

Lincoln Park: In 2007 locals raised money and hired local artist Aileen Baar to create a design for the broad steps. Her Beaux-Arts–inspired creation, with a floral motif, has been described as a colorful rug rolling toward walkers.

HIDDEN CITY

WHAT Stairs of San Francisco

WHERE Hidden all over the city.

COST Free

PRO TIP *Stairway Walks in San Francisco* by Mary Burk and Adah Bakalinksy is a comprehensive guide.

If you're going to Coit Tower, walk the Jack Early stairway. It's called a park but it's really a stairway Early built with railroad ties so walkers could appreciate the bay view.

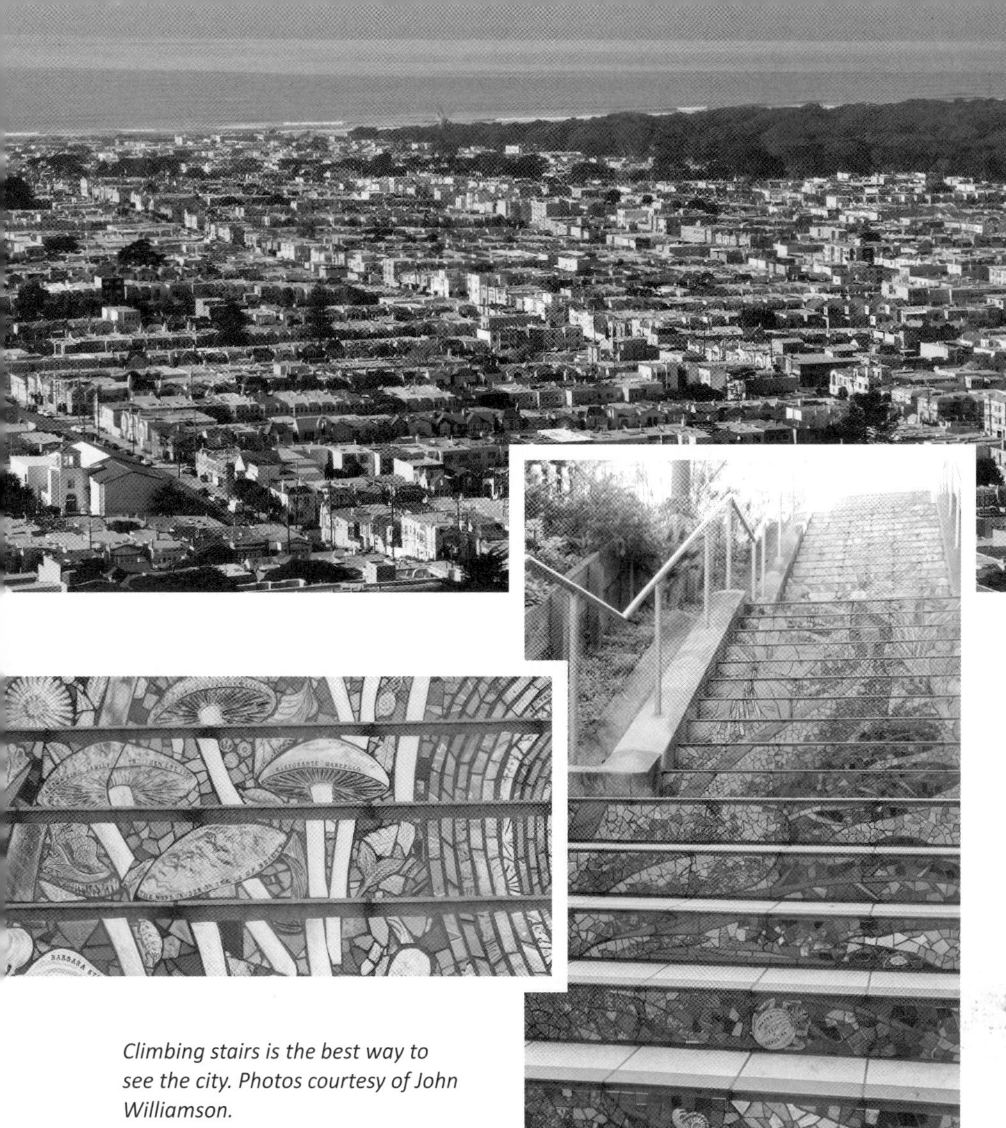

Climbing stairs is the best way to see the city. Photos courtesy of John Williamson.

Lyon Street: This ritzy Pacific Heights stairway, lined with manicured shrubbery, has million-dollar views of the Bay and the Palace of Fine Arts gold dome. Along the way you'll pass a giant heart, part of a fundraising campaign for SF General Hospital.

Sand Ladder: To give you an idea how difficult these sand covered stairs are to climb, they're included on the triathlon circuit. Part of the Pacific Coast Trail, they lead to Baker Beach, which has a nude section. (You've been forewarned.)

19 LEANING TOWER OF SAN FRANCISCO

Why are tenants of a luxury skyscraper suing?

San Francisco is built on the dreams and dust of Gold Rush miners, and some high rollers recently discovered that it can be a weak foundation.

In 2009, well-heeled residents, including Joe Montana, lined up to buy luxury condos at the new Millennium Tower. The swanky skyscraper had million-dollar views, a private bar on the top floor, a wine locker, a Michael Mina restaurant, and a concierge. If it seems too good to be true, it was. A year later the fifty-eight-story building started sinking and tilting. One of the residents videotaped a marble rolling across his floor to show the slant and it became national news.

To date the Millennium has sunk sixteen inches and leans fourteen inches to the west, according to the *San Francisco Chronicle*. Much of the city is built on landfill, and critics say Millennium should have drilled into bedrock. On the other hand, Millennium says construction of the adjacent Transbay Transit Center weakened the soil. If the tower does collapse, it will fall on the new Salesforce skyscraper next door, the largest building west of the Mississippi. Lawsuits are flying back and forth like the green parrots of Telegraph Hill. With their condo prices also falling, homeowners are joining the fray. Residents

---

In 2010 a real life Spiderman scaled the building's exterior. "Skyscraper Man" said he was drawing attention to the difficulty of rescuing people in a skyscraper.

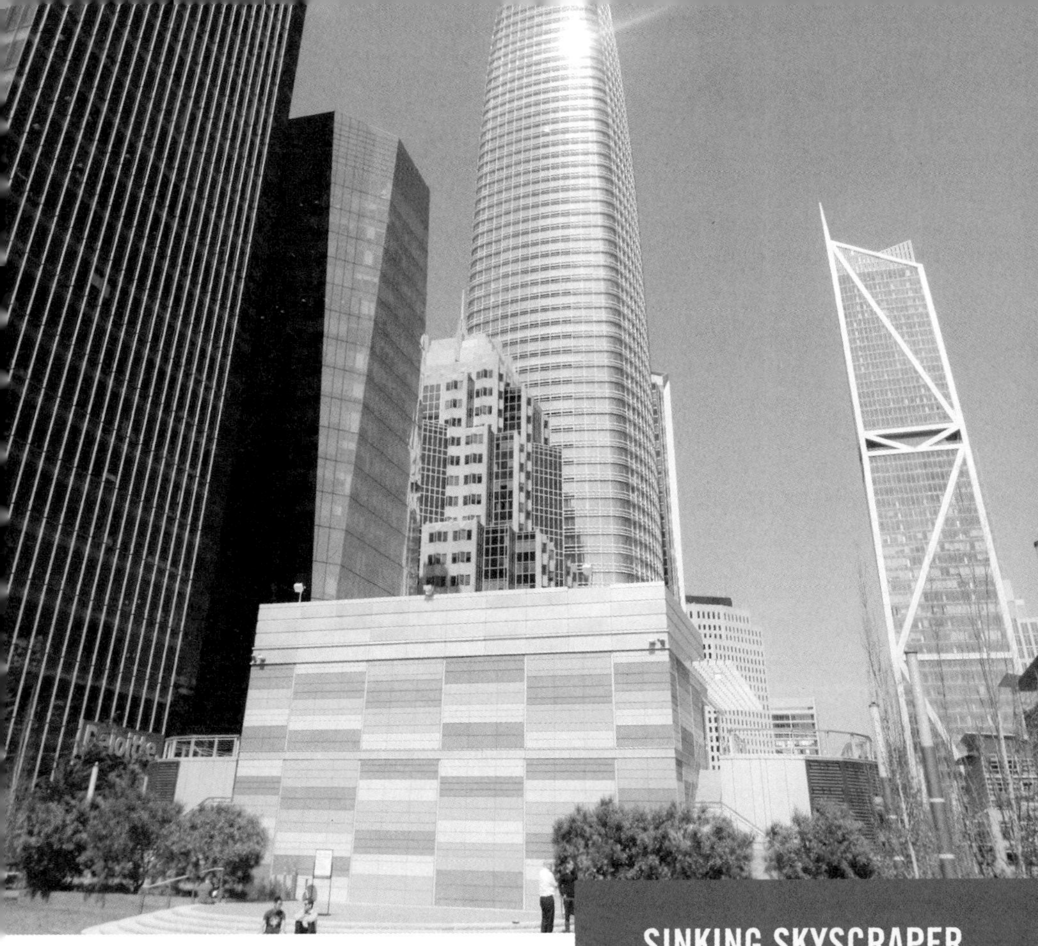

The POPOS here is one of the best in the city. Photo courtesy of John Williamson.

want developers to spend $100 million to drill fifty new steel and concrete piles into bedrock.

Meanwhile San Francisco's version of the Leaning Tower of Pisa has become a tourist attraction even though they can't see the slant and they can't get too close. Scaffolding was put in place to protect the lookie-loos after two windows burst.

SINKING SKYSCRAPER

WHAT Millenium Tower

WHERE 301 Mission St.

COST Free

PRO TIP It has a large POPOS (privately owned public open space) next to a restaurant.

20 BACK TO THE FUTURE

Why is a new ferry getting national attention?

The best way to see San Francisco is by leaving it . . . on a ferry with a view of our unique skyline. The only thing marring your scenic, tranquil ride might be the noise and smell from a diesel engine . . . until now.

Red and White Fleet has invested in a six-hundred-passenger hybrid electric ferry, the first of its kind in the United States. The *Enhydra*, which means sea otter, is a boat that's similar to a Prius, says Tom Escher, chairman of Red and White Fleet. After being plugged in at the dock the ship can cruise for more than two hours. And like a sea otter, *Enhydra* glides through the Bay silently and gracefully.

This innovative boat, with an aluminum hull, was constructed under the watchful eye of the Coast Guard. It's more expensive to build than a regular ferry but Escher is willing to take the financial gamble. "Anyone who is the first in an industry is taking a chance but we're taking more of a chance if we don't do something about pollution."

Escher plans to have all of the Red and White Fleet vessels become zero emission by 2025 and he envisions a day when all the ferries will be using his charging stations at the docks.

The Red and White Fleet is the only ferry with an audio tour in sixteen languages.

With this quiet ferry boat ride you can enjoy the scenery.

The maritime industry has been slow to adopt green technology according to Escher and he wants to change that. "We're going back to the future," laughs Escher. "When my grandfather, Tom Crowley, started the company in 1892, he only had a rowboat and we're aiming for that same zero emissions."

WHEN ZERO IS 100 PERCENT

WHAT A hybrid ferry

WHERE Fisherman's Wharf, Red and White Fleet, Pier 431/2, foot of Taylor St.

COST Cruises range from $33.00 to $70.00 per person.

PRO TIP Check GoldStar.com for discount tickets.

21 MURALS WITH A MESSAGE

What part of town has the most outdoor art?

Skyscrapers and asphalt make cities dark. Add fog to the mix and it's no wonder San Francisco is called the "cool gray city of love". So when you come across streets lined with wildly colorful vivid works of art you're transported to a different world.

This is the Mission, traditional home of the Latino-American population who began painting murals outdoors in the late 1960s, when the new Politec mural paints, formulated in Mexico, became available in the United States.

Hundreds of buildings and fences are decorated with murals of Latino leaders, farmers, Carnaval dancers, parrots, warrior women, and the Virgin Mary.

THE PEOPLE'S ART

WHAT Mission Murals

WHERE All over the Mission District

COST Free

PRO TIP If you're short on time, take a walk down Clarion and Balmy Alleys where murals cover almost every available surface.

Some of the more notable include:

The *MaestraPeace* mural on the Women's Building at 3453 18th Street. This mural has received international recognition, in part because it was a multi-cultural, multi-generational

---

Mexican artist Diego Rivera was making political statements with murals back in the 1930s. You can see them at SF City College and the Art Institute.

Women are frequent subjects of murals in the Mission.

collaboration between seven women artists and more than 100 female volunteers.

The *Carnaval Mural*, also known as “Golden Dreams of the Mission,” on 24th Street. It blends into the architecture so well that people think the building is a Victorian.

If you’re inspired to create your own murals the Precita Eyes Mural and Visitor Center can teach you. Everyone here is an artist as well as a teacher and, in addition to lessons, they offer tours that cover the murals’ cultural and historical significance.

22 GHOSTLY LANDMARK

Why is a funeral home a tourist attraction?

The Columbarium is a story of reincarnation. This copper-domed neoclassical building survived the 1906 earthquake only to fall into disrepair.

When San Francisco was rapidly expanding in the early 1900s it needed land and outlawed funeral homes and cemeteries, moving bodies to nearby Colma. There was an exception: the Columbarium, where the deceased were above ground in urns.

Over the years this building was abandoned until the Neptune Society purchased it in 1980 and restored it to its original beauty. Today the Columbarium is a San Francisco landmark as well as a functioning funeral home.

Located in a residential cul-de-sac in the Richmond District, tourists come to see the atrium surrounded by ornate stained-glass windows, but the main attraction is the tiny glass cubes filled with artifacts of loved ones. There's a hula dancer, Christmas tree lights, and an urn that plays "How Dry I Am" next to a Johnny Walker bottle. The niches reveal the personalities of loved ones and also tell the city's story.

The people who built San Francisco rest here, the same names you'll see on street signs like Haight, Hayes, and Folsom. One of the founders of Wells Fargo Bank is here along with famous names who sold two of San Francisco's favorite beverages, a Folger coffee heir and a brewmaster from Anchor Brewing Company. More recently, local celebrities have made their final homes here: the ashes of the San Francisco Brown

---

The Columbarium is the only non-denominational burial place in San Francisco and the only one that still has space.

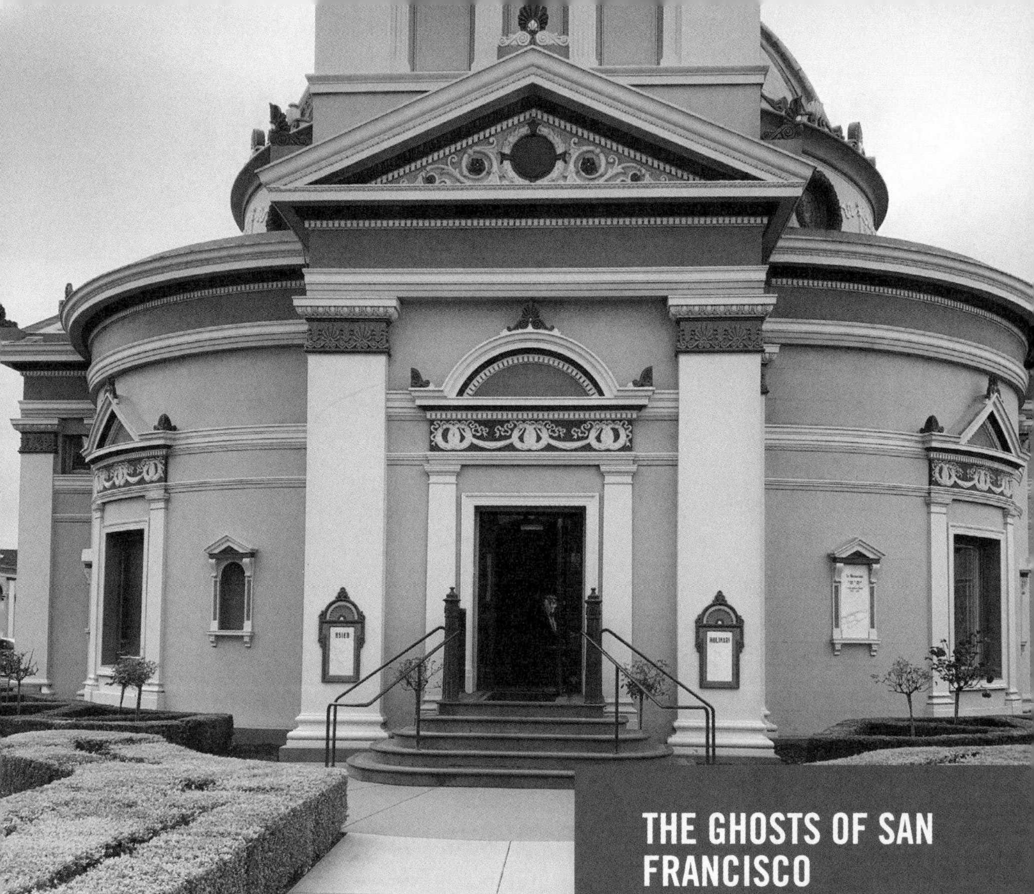

The Columbarium is frequently booked for private events. Photo courtesy of John Williamson.

THE GHOSTS OF SAN FRANCISCO

WHAT An eternal historical attraction

WHERE 1 Loraine Court

COST Free

PRO TIP You can visit anytime on your own but it's worthwhile to make an appointment for the free tour with Emmitt Watson.

twins (who always dressed identically) and Chet Helms, father of the "Summer of Love," share space with a memorial for slain supervisor and gay rights activist Harvey Milk.

Emmitt Watson, who was largely responsible for restoring the building, also leads tours and is in charge of interments. It started as a job, but now it's Emmitt's passion. "I tell people, 'I can't do anything for you but I can take care of your loved one.'" He's seen ghosts but says they're friendly, and he's very proud of the gardens because they bring life to the funeral home.

23 SLOWING DOWN TIME

What is a giant sundial doing in a cul-de-sac?

It's one of those marketing ploys that will go down in history . . . building the largest sundial in the world to attract homebuyers. Strange as it sounds, in 1913 the Urban Realty Improvement Company thought a giant white sundial would increase home sales at Ingleside Terraces. At that time, home prices ranged from $6,000 to $20,000.

They held a gala event (ironically, at night) where a Coast Guard Auxiliary Band played and children dressed as water nymphs unveiled the "park" which contained Greek columns, a fountain, a reflecting pool, and the sundial. The pamphlet for the event said the sundial "bridges a limpid pool wherein two bronze seals spoon and form the base of the fountain that plays day and night. Running around the stone curb of the pool is a circlet of gorgeous purple and yellow pansies. Then comes the broad dial marked with Roman numerals."

The site was formerly a racetrack and nearby Urbano street follows that loop exactly. The Ingleside racetrack was a major attraction in 1895 when at least 8000 people came out for the opening and Southern Pacific railway built a special line to the track. By 1905 it closed down due to lack of attendance and the space, including jockey houses and stables, became a refugee camp for earthquake survivors.

There is now a much larger sundial in Bay View/Hunters Point (its pointer is seventy-eight feet long), so maybe the Ingleside realtors were ahead of their time in recognizing the importance of public art.

Reportedly there is a jockey home left over from the racetrack at 280 Byxbee.

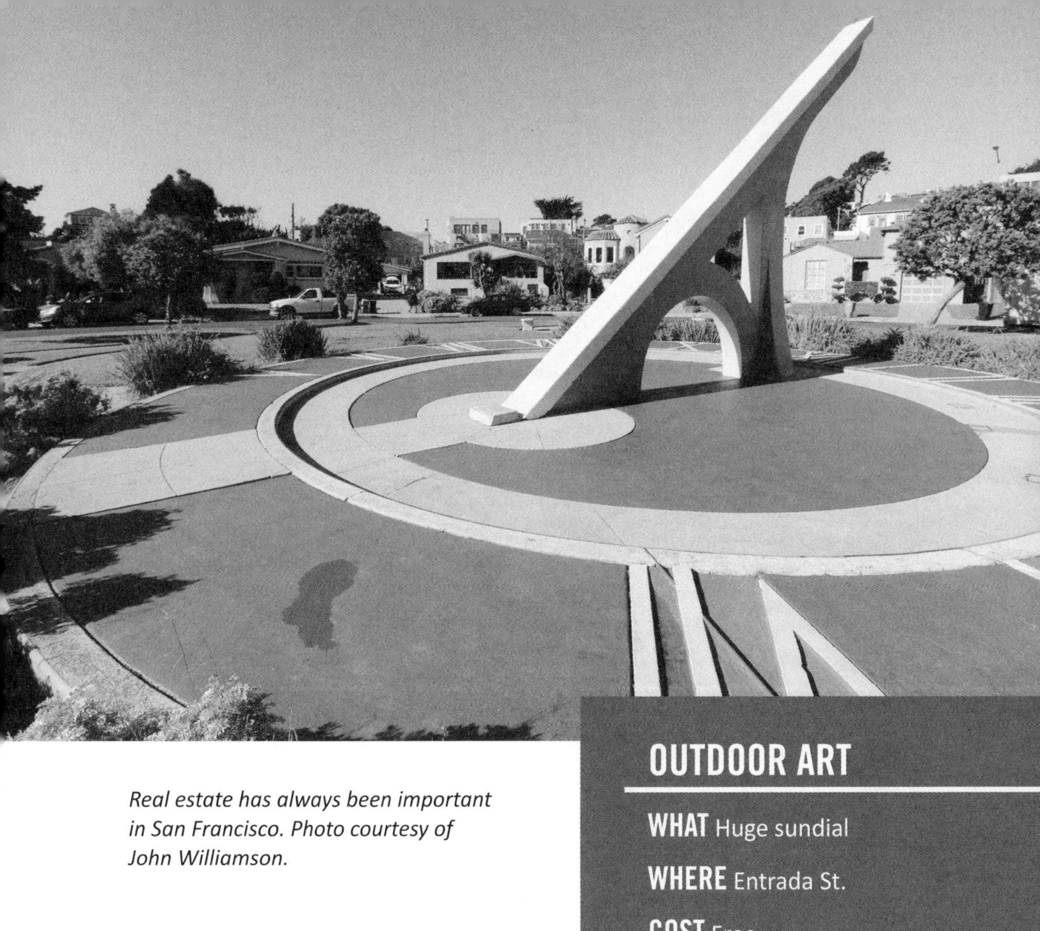

Real estate has always been important in San Francisco. Photo courtesy of John Williamson.

OUTDOOR ART

WHAT Huge sundial

WHERE Entrada St.

COST Free

PRO TIP End your day watching the sunset at nearby Ocean Beach.

24 CAMERA READY

What's the largest space in the world dedicated to photography?

Hint: it's in a warehouse with minimal signage, there's never a line to enter, and it's free. Pier 24 Photography is not your usual museum.

PHOTO OP

WHAT A photography museum, the only free private museum in the city

WHERE Pier 24

COST Free, but you must make an appointment online at https://pier24.org/visit

PRO TIP Want to know the names of the photographers usually posted next to the artwork? The museum sells catalogs of every exhibit they've displayed that contains that info . . . perfect coffee table books.

Andrew and Mary Pilara created this private museum and opened it to the public in 2010 when their photography collection outgrew their home. The Diane Arbus retrospective at San Francisco Museum of Modern Art in 2003 inspired them to acquire their first piece of photography. That first photograph has grown to a collection of over 5,500 photographs by international artists. In addition to the permanent collection, Pier 24 Photography stages exhibitions, often including emerging photographers.

The building itself begs to be photographed. Located between gritty industrial buildings directly under the Bay Bridge, visitors can snap shots of sea lions surrounding sailboats.

Guests can spend up to two hours in the museum, but they must make an appointment. Pier 24 limits the number of guests because they want everyone to have a relaxed visit.

The photo museum begs for Instagram pics. Photos courtesy of Tom O'Connor.

Everything is designed to help you concentrate on the photos. It's a self-guided tour, the booklet intentionally has minimal text, and the photographs are not cluttered by signs naming the artist, date, or where the photo took place.

Start your own photo collection by walking through San Francisco's neighborhoods and snapping shots.

25 TECHIES TAKE A TIME OUT

A Café with a Cause

Snapchat, Instagram, Twitter, Facebook: the special moments of our lives are posted there . . . for a moment. Some techies find this disposable society so alarming they're promoting long-term thinking by creating a "Stonehenge" clock built to last 10,000 years. The Long Now foundation was created two decades ago by engineer Danny Hillis, musician Brian Eno, and Stewart Brand, a Renaissance man who hung out with the Merry Pranksters in the '60s. Amazon CEO Jeff Bezos joined their cause by donating a remote piece of land in Texas, where the clock is undergoing construction.

Prototypes of the timepiece are on display at the Interval Café in Fort Mason, the Long Now headquarters. A 1930s Marine garage that used to fix Army boats has been converted into a bar that looks like a steampunk library. The space contains: a pendulum clock under a glass dome, tables mounted on clock gears, a spiral stairway lined with books, and a robotic blackboard that draws geeky art. Numbered bottles of aged liquor created just for the Café hang from the ceiling, and

SLOWING DOWN TIME

WHAT The Interval

WHERE 2 Marina Blvd.

COST Free to enter: the menu is affordable

PRO TIP The food menu is limited but next door the renowned vegetarian restaurant Greens has sandwiches to go.

Be sure to go in the back room and look up: there's a spiral image of the clock under construction in Texas.

The Interval has a private back you can reserve. Top photo courtesy of Christopher Michael, right photo courtesy of Ruth Carlson.

the bartender references a Rolodex to find customers' pre-paid vintages.

"Ideas ferment in a café culture," says Michael McElligott, Interval spokesman. "This space represents what Long Now is all about with artifacts, books and a sense of history." Even the bar is educational; the menu lists the origins of every cocktail. Many nights the café turns into a salon with speakers on topics such as climate change, science fiction, and art.

26 THE PLINY PHENOMENON

What local beer has international cult status?

Every February, like men buying their sweethearts roses for Valentine's Day at the last minute, beer aficionados from around the globe line up for eight hours, often in the rain, for a chance to quaff Pliny the Younger. You can't buy this beer in bottles, cans, or growlers; the only way you can taste this limited release is by visiting the Russian River Brewing Company (RRBC) in Santa Rosa where patrons are limited to three glasses over three hours and when the day's allocation runs out, the brewpub closes. Let's raise a glass to the twelve thousand people who visited Sonoma County for last year's release and spent $3.4 million!

What's so great about a beer that people camp out overnight to taste it? RRBC say it's a very time-consuming, extremely expensive beer to make, and probably the first-ever triple IPA.

Pliny the Elder, however, is sold by the bottle to select stores. Delivered fresh weekly it usually sells out immediately, and customers are often limited to two bottles per person, a

BEER NUTS

WHAT Pliny the Younger

WHERE Russian River Brewing Company

COST $5.25 for a half pint

PRO TIP RRBC just opened another tasting room in nearby Windsor that will also release Pliny the Younger.

In a time when microbrews are selling out to corporations, Russian River Brewing Company is still owned and run by the same husband and wife team who started the business, Vinnie and Natalie Cilurzo.

Anchor Steam was the first microbrewery in the Bay Area.

policy not endorsed by RRBC. It was rated the number one IPA in the nation for eight consecutive years, until 2017 when it came in second to Bell's Two Hearted Ale from Michigan.

Just to make Pliny even more unusual, RRBC chose a Latin name. Pliny the Elder was an ancient Roman lawyer and author who was killed in the eruption of Mt. Vesuvius. His nephew, Pliny the Younger, wrote letters that described the eruptions and are now valued historical documents. While most people, including the staff, pronounce the beer "ply-nee" (rhymes with *tiny*), the Latin pronunciation is "plinn-ee," rhymes with *tinny*.

27 CREATIVITY EXPLORED

Who is the surprise winner of the award for Best Art Gallery in San Francisco?

San Francisco is an artsy town. We have the Museum of Modern Art, the De Young Museum, the Legion of Honor, murals in the Mission, a Cartoon Museum, art galleries galore, and Creativity Explored.

Never heard of the last one? You've probably seen their creations: wild patterns for fashion house Commes de Garcons; colorful illustrations on Google's self-driving cars; designs for CB2 furniture, a mural at the Salesforce Tower, and even whimsical drawings on Recchiuti chocolate.

As impressive as this resume is, it's even more impressive when you learn the art was created by adults with developmental disabilities. An art gallery and studio in the Mission District, it's a model program for non-profits around the world.

Thirty-five years ago, Florence Ludins-Katz, an artist, and her husband, Elias Katz, a psychiatrist, dreamed up a place where disabled adults could become independent by selling their artwork and express themselves in the process. "Even if they can't speak, they can communicate through art," explains Paul Moshammer, the studio director.

Artists get half of all the proceeds from their sales and buyers know they're helping a non-profit . . . but that's not why they're lining up to purchase the paintings, the art is amazing.

In 2019 Creativity Explored will begin a program where anyone can take classes from professional artists. Just don't be surprised if the regular students teach you more than the instructor.

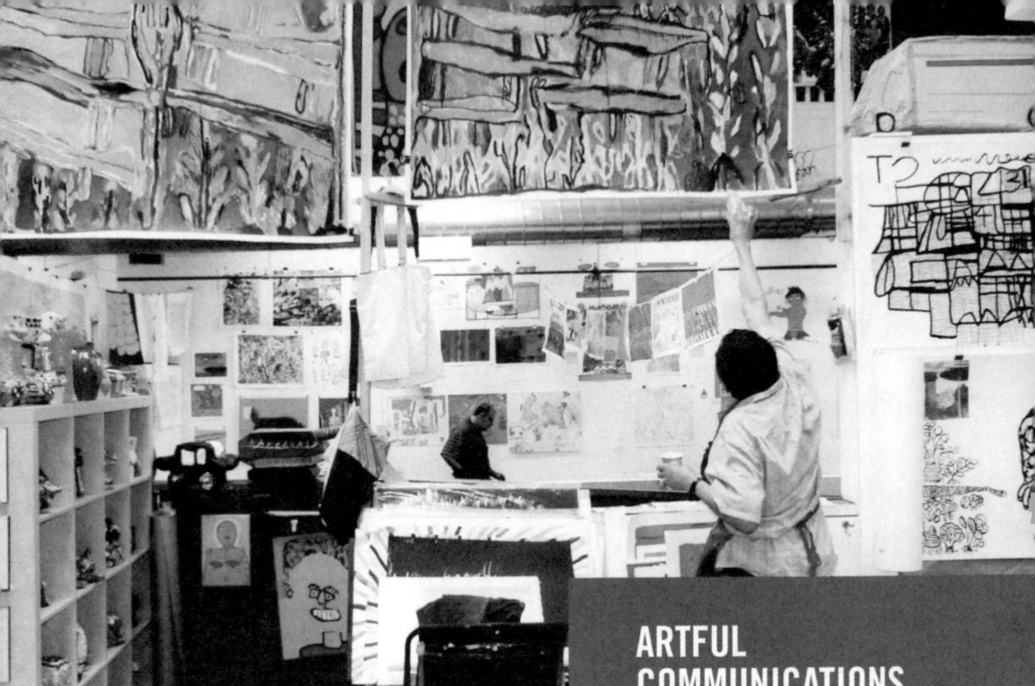

Creativity Explored inspires visitors to be more artistic.

ARTFUL COMMUNICATIONS

WHAT An art studio and gallery for adults with developmental disabilities

WHERE 3245 16th St.

COST Free entry to the studio and gallery. Prices range from $5 to $200.

PRO TIP The gallery holds several exhibitions annually and a gala fundraiser in April.

The UC Berkeley Art Museum showcased pieces from Creativity Explored and so did galleries in New Zealand and Australia. "It changes people's assumptions about disability," says Executive Director Linda Johnson.

The store sells watercolors, ceramics, sculptures, clothing, notebooks, stationery, and tote bags . . . and they are affordable.

Unlike most artists who create in solitude, Creativity Explored painters welcome people watching their creative process. Johnson has noticed that "people fall in love when they visit, there's an instant connection."

"Everyone has the ability to create and working in the studio with professional art instructors builds their confidence," adds Moshammer.

28 TWAIN'S TUMULTUOUS TIMES

How did San Francisco make Mark Twain famous?

"The coldest winter I ever spent was a summer in San Francisco." Everyone loves to quote this Mark Twain quip, but did he really say it? "Doubtful," says Ben Griffin, editor of the Mark Twain papers at UC Berkeley's Bancroft Library. "He did say something about cold weather, but it was in reference to Paris."

We'll never know for sure, but we do know that the two years Samuel Clemens (aka Mark Twain) spent in San Francisco were pivotal to his career. For one thing he met a saloon owner and fireman named Tom Sawyer. After the book was a success Sawyer hung a banner outside his bar reading: "I'm the Original Tom Sawyer."

Clemens was a reporter for *The Daily Morning Call* newspaper that coincidentally was next door to his friend Bret Harte's office at the Mint. A precursor to San Francisco columnist Herb Caen, Twain covered the theater, restaurants, and high society. In one hilarious post, he wrote about visiting the Cliff House at 4 a.m. to avoid traffic. His carriage was indeed alone on the foggy roads but Clemens was freezing and could barely see. He recommended visiting any time after 7 a.m. when you couldn't fail to enjoy yourself, although he was disappointed in the seals that were "writhing and squirming like exaggerated maggots."

After Twain died the vast majority of his papers were bequeathed to Bancroft Library.

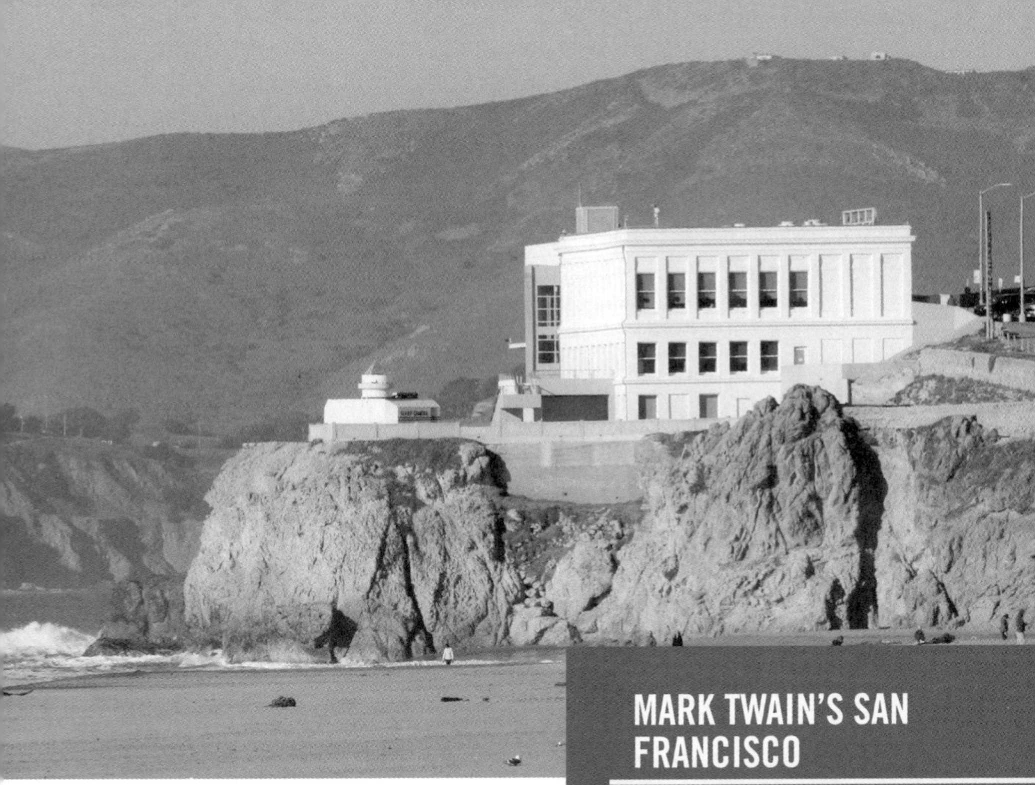

MARK TWAIN'S SAN FRANCISCO

WHAT Cliff House

WHERE 1090 Point Lobos Ave.

COST Free to enter. There are several restaurants with varying prices.

PRO TIP Don't miss the paintings of the Fleishhacker saltwater swimming pool.

Allegedly, Twain hated Angels Camp, land of the frog-jumping contest. Photo courtesy of John Williamson.

Allegedly, Twain did not let facts get in the way of a good story, which led to the first and last time he was fired. A tumultuous time in his life, he spent a night in jail for drunk and disorderly conduct that a rival newspaper reveled in reporting. Humiliated, Twain hid out in Angels Camp, where he watched a frog-jumping contest. The New York *Saturday Press* published the story, and Twain found his true calling as a humorous writer.

29 DOGGIE DINER

Why does Treasure Island have three huge dog statues?

San Franciscans love rescue animals, but it's still surprising they found homes for three dachshunds weighing six hundred pounds each. Mannie, Moe, and Jack are fiberglass statues happily living on Treasure Island, the last turnoff on the Bay Bridge before you leave the City.

These special dogs don't need to be walked, and they're always dressed to impress in chef hats and bow ties. Born in 1948, they grew up working, rotating on poles in front of Doggie Diners, a hot dog chain in SF and Oakland. When the restaurants closed in 1986, there were about thirty dog heads but sadly most were thrown away.

Zippy the Pinhead comic strip started a grassroots movement to save the beloved mascot, and the city listened, naming one a landmark and mounting it in the median strip of Sloat Boulevard near Ocean Beach. San Francisco resident John Law rescued three of the constantly smiling dogs who are enjoying retirement posing for Instagram and appearing at non-profit events.

When strong winds knocked the Sloat Boulevard dog's head off its pole, damaging the face, Law was able to lend one of his Treasure Island mascots as a model to the artists doing reconstruction.

Treasure Island was created out of sand for the 1939 World's Fair.

Instead of dalmatians, firefighters on Treasure Island have Doggie Diner heads.

HOT DIGGITY

WHAT Doggie Diner heads

WHERE Treasure Island next to the firehouse or Sloat Boulevard median strip across from the Zoo.

COST Free

PRO TIP There are several wineries and brewpubs along the waterfront you can visit after your Dog Day Afternoon or Three Dog Night.

30 CHRISTMAS CON

Why do hundreds of Santas gather in Union Square each December?

Yes, Virginia, there is a Santa Claus . . . hundreds of them, in fact. If you don't believe me, you will on the first Saturday of December. That's when anyone who believes in Christmas (even for a day), dresses as Santa and gathers around an eighty-three-foot-tall Christmas tree in Union Square.

Now a worldwide phenomenon, the San Francisco performance art group Cacophony Society created SantaCon in 1994. John Law, who cofounded the event with Rob Schmitt, said it began as a whimsical protest against commercialism, inspired by a group of Danish activists. The Danes, dressed as Santas, entered department stores and gave away toys to children. The kids were thrilled until the police arrived, took their toys away, and beat up Santa!

In 1994, SF's first SantaCon was a more subtle statement. "About thirty Santas showed up and we stopped at hotels and department stores singing Christmas carols, changing the lyrics just enough to mess with people in a fun way," laughs Law. Today SantaCon, or Santarchy as some call it, is a flash-mob event where anyone dressed as Santa, Mrs. Claus, an elf, or even a Christmas tree, goes on a pub crawl and spends a lot of time explaining to staring children that they're not the real Santa.

In 1975 the Christmas tree was joined by the first giant public menorah. It was erected with the help of the rock promoter and Holocaust survivor Bill Graham.

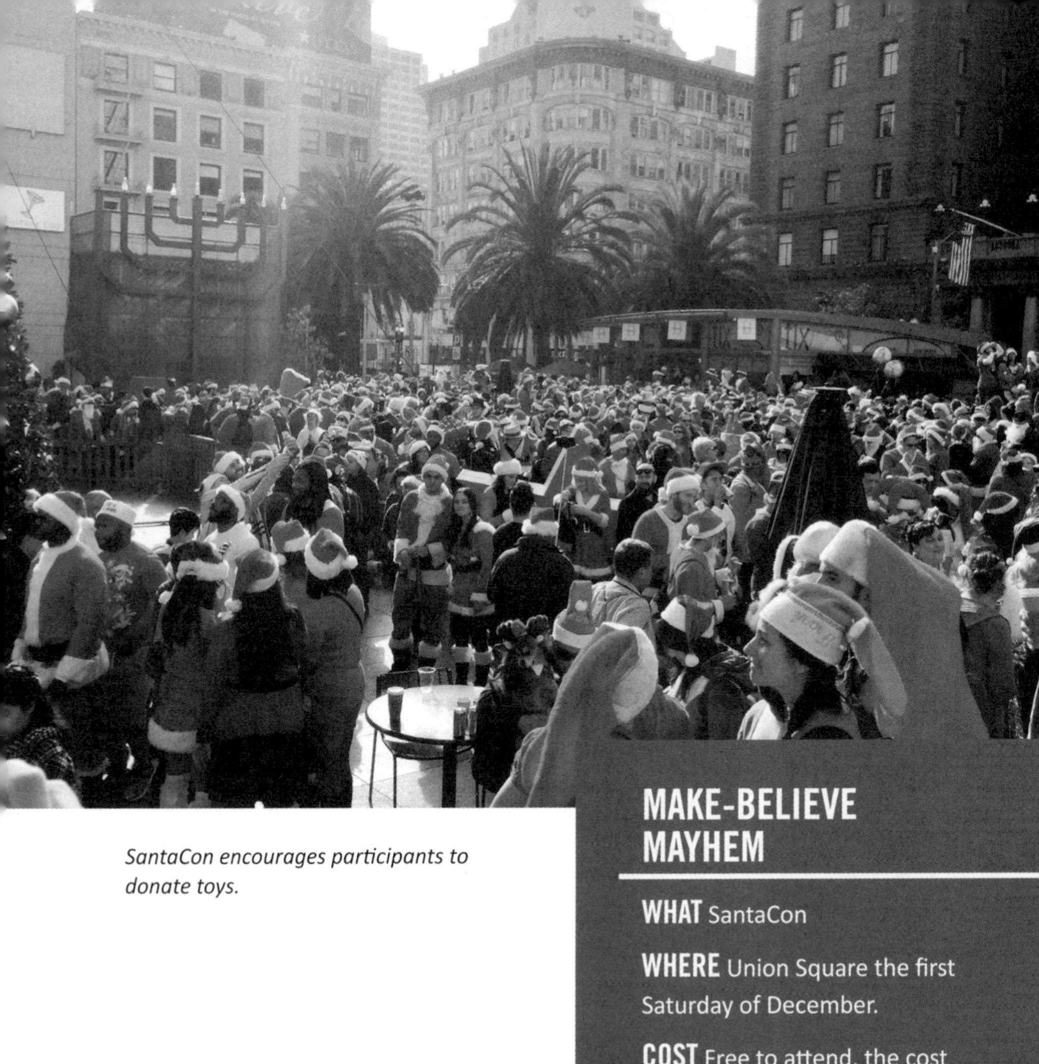

SantaCon encourages participants to donate toys.

MAKE-BELIEVE MAYHEM

WHAT SantaCon

WHERE Union Square the first Saturday of December.

COST Free to attend, the cost of your costume is up to you.

PRO TIP Get your Santa outfit early; they sell out fast in San Francisco.

31 FREE TRIP AROUND THE WORLD

Where did the term "shanghaied" originate?

The Barbary Coast was very tempting for a sailor fresh off the boat. He had his wages in hand and—for the first time in months—saw ladies . . . scantily clad dancing women! It was the perfect place for nefarious "crimps" (the nickname for these unscrupulous kidnappers) to take advantage of the dockhands.

During the gold rush, ships filled with treasure hunters arrived daily but the return voyage was a problem. Skippers had a hard time recruiting sailors who were more interested in the Barbary Coast and mining for gold than getting back on a boat. Saloons, often in cahoots with boardinghouses, drugged the sailors' drinks and when they were unconscious, dropped them through a trap door into a waiting boat. Back then North Beach was actually a beach—although it was later covered with landfill—and many bars were built over the water. Duped sailors woke up on ships and had no choice but to work.

Ships were often headed to Shanghai, which is where the word shanghaied originated. Once the sailors arrived in China it was difficult to get a return ride, so they ended up traveling around the globe to get back to San Francisco, spending years at sea.

Pacific Avenue was called Terrific Street during the Gold Rush days because of its abundance of brothels, dance halls, and saloons—all likely places to get shanghaied.

Tour the schooners at Hyde St. Pier. Photo courtesy of John Williamson.

SHANGHAI SPOT

WHAT A tunnel used to shanghai sailors

WHERE Hippodrome building, now the Artist and Craftsman Supply store, 555 Pacific Avenue, lower floor.

COST Free

PRO TIP To add to their historical appeal, many bars in San Francisco today also claim they were used for shanghaiing, The Saloon and Comstock among them.

One notorious kidnapper was James Kelly, known as Shanghai Kelly. Legend has it that one day three ships were in urgent need of sailors, and Kelly aimed to make a fortune by staffing all three. He chartered a paddlewheel and invited everyone along the waterfront to a free party celebrating his birthday. Dozens of men showed up, and when they passed out from the drugged drinks, Kelly handed them off to the ships' captains. Bill Pickelhaupt, author of *Shanghaied in San Francisco*, sheds doubt on this story, but it's such a part of San Francisco lore that there's even a saloon on Polk Street called Shanghai Kelly. Rumor has it Kelly was forced to quit when he was shanghaied!

32 PAGE TURNER

Who is keeping print alive?

New York has fashion, LA has movies, and San Francisco has writers. Perhaps you've heard of a few: Mark Twain, Dashiell Hammett, Jack Kerouac, Maya Angelou . . . the list is as long as the Salesforce Tower is tall.

So it makes sense that we're home to one of the last working metal type foundries in the world. Mackenzie & Harris (M&H), in the Presidio, is a working museum. This time machine makes books the old-fashioned way: type is cast from molten metal and set into pages. Then pages are printed onto letterpresses, hand sewn into blocks, and bound onto boards, and packed into cases.

M&H is part of Arion Press, a fine printing house that produces just three books a year for its subscribers. Artisans at Arion Press undergo years of apprenticeship and learn arcane techniques like dampening handmade paper overnight. The latest manuscript is stories by Oscar Wilde with a foreword written by his grandson.

Arion has drawers of irreplaceable handset type and proof presses—including the one Mark Twain invested in and lost his money on—that were being thrown out in the 1950s. Those presses were rescued by beat writers who used them to

---

Walking around the city you'll notice alleys with names like Saroyan and Jack London. Poet Lawrence Ferlinghetti, owner of City Lights Bookstore, wanted to name streets after local authors but residents protested. He had better luck with sparsely populated alleyways.

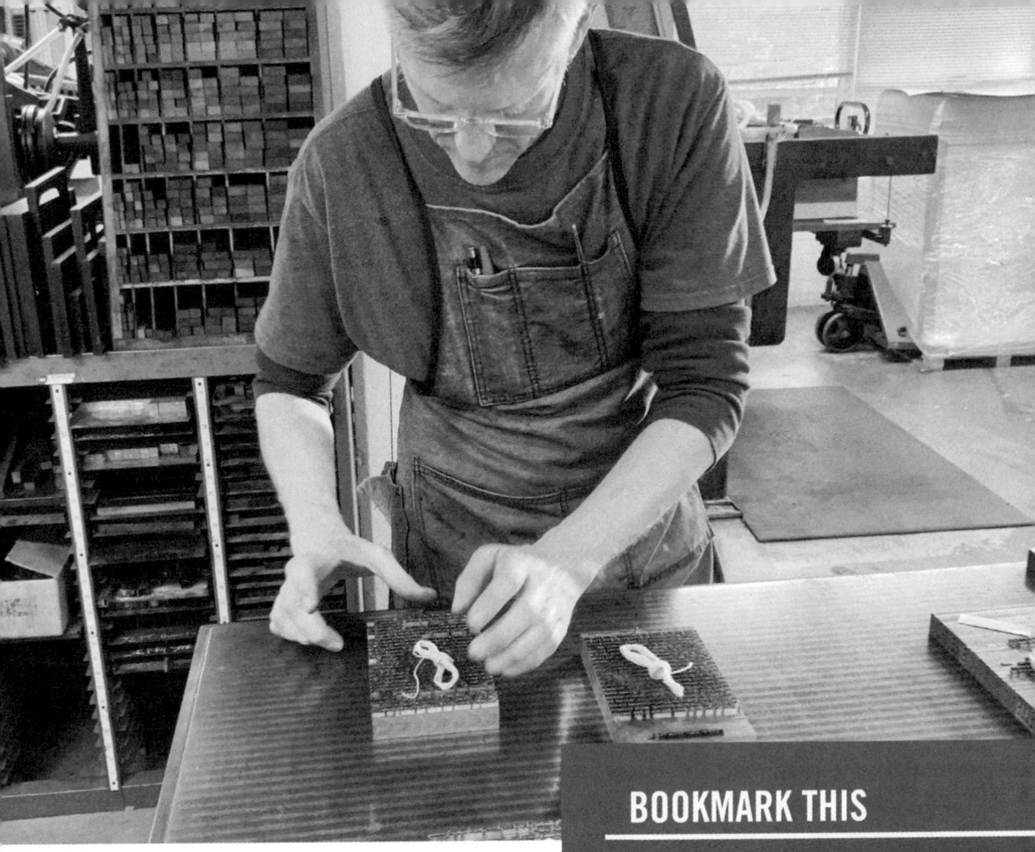

Bibliophiles should note that the San Francisco public library has an annual book sale each year at Fort Mason.

independently publish their own books, spawning a whole beatnik movement.

San Francisco weather, like that in Venice and Florence, is also a reason printing flourished here. The humidity makes it easier to print.

BOOKMARK THIS

WHAT Tours of Arion Press, Thursdays at 3:30

WHERE 1802 Hayes, The Presidio

COST $10.00

PRO TIP Arrive before the tour to look around at exhibits of their latest books in the gallery.

33 SEADOG CHAPEL

Why is there a tiny church along Fisherman's Wharf?

In between the fishing boats, seafood restaurants, and tourist traps, there's a small brown building hiding in plain sight. St. John's Oratory, or the Fishermen's and Seamen's Memorial Chapel, is a Roman Catholic church built in 1981 to honor those lost at sea. Interestingly, the chapel was built on the site of the old Coast Guard building, former home to the first responders when people are missing at sea.

While the wooden structure is unimpressive from the outside, the interior has a stained-glass window featuring a ship's wheel, a crystal chandelier with fifteen candelabra lights representing the Rosary, and an antique banner depicting the patron saint of Sicilian fishermen, Madonna del Lume. Over two hundred plaques memorializing fishermen who died at sea line the walls. In 2006 a campanile was added topped by a bell saved from a ship dating to 1860. The campanile rings every day at 9 a.m., noon, and 6 p.m.

It's the only place in the Bay Area where you can hear Gregorian chants and a full traditional Latin Mass (pre-Vatican II) just like the services the original Sicilian immigrant fishermen attended. Any male can join in the Gregorian chants—no singing ability required—and you don't have to be Catholic; just show up at the practice held at 9 a.m. every Sunday. The ancient melodies are then chanted for real shortly afterwards at 9:30 a.m.

The chapel is the only building that has been added to the wharf since 1950.

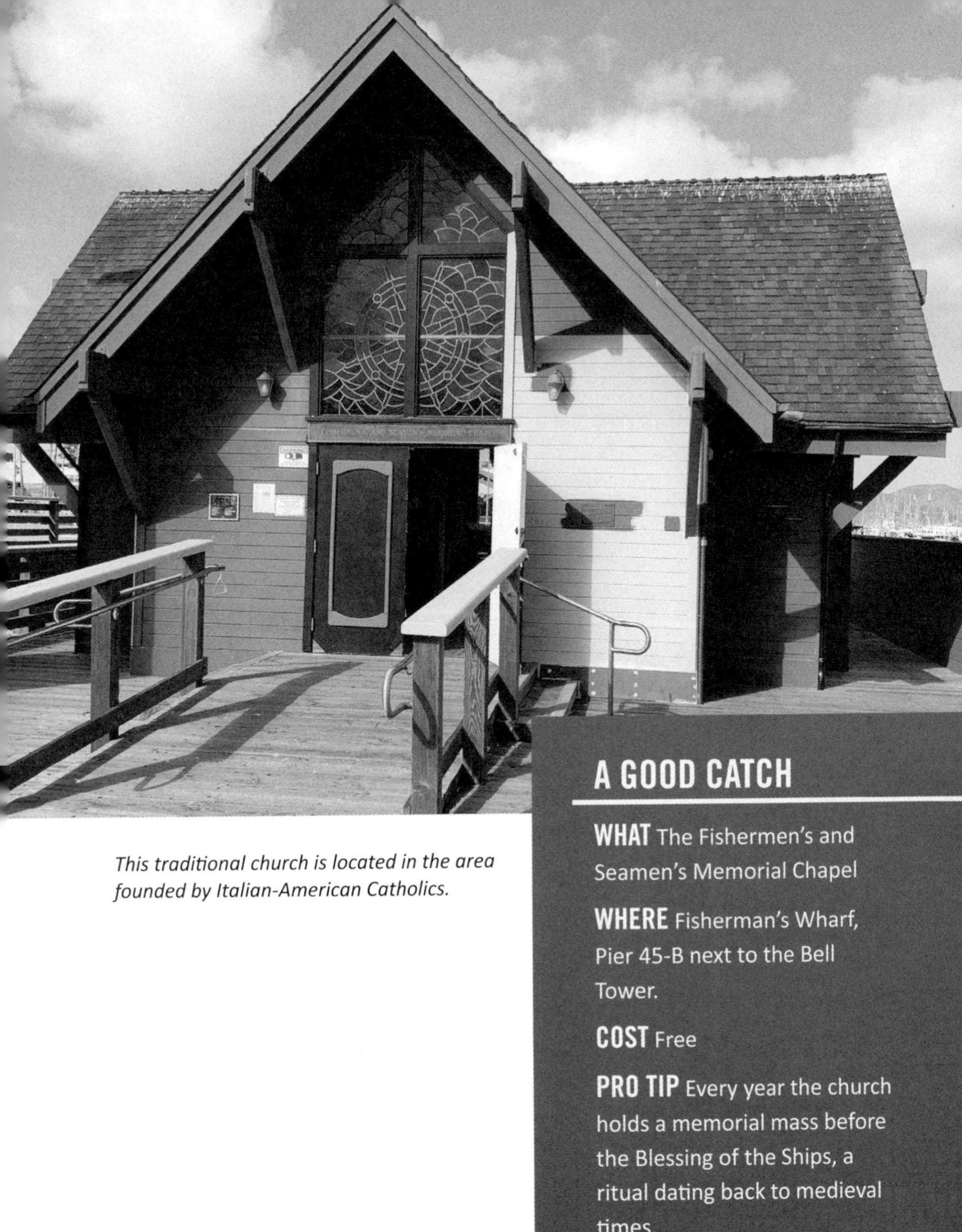

This traditional church is located in the area founded by Italian-American Catholics.

A GOOD CATCH

WHAT The Fishermen's and Seamen's Memorial Chapel

WHERE Fisherman's Wharf, Pier 45-B next to the Bell Tower.

COST Free

PRO TIP Every year the church holds a memorial mass before the Blessing of the Ships, a ritual dating back to medieval times.

34 ART HOUSE

Why are people taking tours in a residential neighborhood?

Enter the Gregangelo Museum at your own risk; you may never want to leave. It's a fun house for adults, with hidden doors, circus paintings, and spinning time capsules. Located in a sleepy neighborhood with manicured lawns, only the porch indicates what's inside. Every inch is covered; the colorful broken tiles and jewels with an orange sand dollar on the ceiling are just a hint of what's to come.

CRAZY CIRCUS HOUSE

WHAT Gregangelo Museum Tours

WHERE 225 San Leandro Way

COST $55–65 lower level, $85 for both lower and upper levels.

PRO TIP If you go on the upstairs tour be prepared for crawling, bright lights, and some cramped spaces.

It's like entering a kaleidoscope. Everywhere you look there's color . . . on disco balls, circus scenes, and conceptual art pieces. Each of the twenty-seven rooms has a theme, including Arabian nights, a spaceship, a bathroom under the sea, and a pink stuffed-animal cave. Salvador Dali would feel right at home.

You're required to relinquish your phone during the tour so you can fully immerse yourself in Gregangelo Herrera's world. An artist, he created this adult fun house with the help of his friends. "Everyone involved with this house is an artist. Even

---

Gregangelo also has a circus called Velocity, which performs for special events throughout the city.

One visit is not enough to see all the art in this house.

the plumber is an artist," he laughs. "People ask me how I planned this house, there was no plan," says the man nicknamed Whirling Dervish. "Artists just kept adding on to it, and it's still changing. There's someone painting a mural right now."

The tour is a combination art appreciation class, science lesson, and therapy session, as the guide explains the meanings behind the rooms while performing magic tricks in between.

35 THE HUMAN LIE DETECTOR

Who can read your mind?

The first clue that this won't be a normal evening: entering the former speakeasy decorated with tapestries, low couches, and ornate pillows. It's akin to a green room where stars gather before a show—and soon you're one of them!

The audience is part of the act in the intimate Marrakech Magic Theater. Wearing his trademark fedora, Jay Alexander interacts with the audience and invites people to the stage, where he reads their minds.

He's a magician who's not afraid to spill his secrets. "It's in the nose," he says, explaining that everyone has "tells." An expert on micro-expressions, he notices tiny clues most of us miss . . . a glance, a head tilt, a voice change. He's so good that one participant was convinced the people he randomly selected were pre-selected. They weren't—I was one of them.

More than a magic act, Alexander is a comic, mind reader, psychologist, and philosopher. At the end of the show he talks about overcoming dyslexia and a speech impediment through magic and encourages audience members to support children's dreams.

His passion was ignited when he stumbled across a trunk filled with magic tricks in his grandfather's attic. In any other home this would be unusual, but Alexander's grandfather was the legendary vaudeville performer, Gentleman Ben Darwin. At just fourteen Alexander became the youngest person to receive the Society of American Magicians Gold Medal of Honor and he's never looked back.

Celebrity clients include the Rolling Stones and the late Robin Williams.

A magician who tells you his secrets!

He's been on national TV but credits word of mouth as central to his success. "I'm the highest-rated performer on Yelp that no one has heard of," he laughs. "People say, 'I've lived here forever and never heard of this show.'"

A popular cruise ship performer, he burned out after visiting thirty-five countries in one year, and decided to purchase the Marrakech Magic Theater.

HOW TO MAKE THE BLUES DISAPPEAR

WHAT A magical performance

WHERE Marrakech Magic Theater

COST $45.00

PRO TIP The building is also home to one of California's oldest Moroccan restaurants. Arrive early to sample their authentic appetizers and signature cocktails.

36 FIRST SKYSCRAPER?

Why do architects love the Hallidie Building?

In 1918 appalled critics nicknamed it "the camouflage building," according to Rick Evans, an architect historian who leads tours throughout the city. The futuristic Hallidie Building, located in the middle of a block that survived the 1906 quake, shook up the status quo.

A significant investment for the University of California, Berkeley, they hired architect Willis Polk. UC had a limited budget, which turned out to be a good thing. Cost cutting led Polk to dream up an innovative design with glass curtain walls, the first of its kind in the nation, and a precursor to skyscrapers. Polk softened the glass grid with gold ornamentation and even made the fire escapes attractive, topping them with ornate balconies. (Though only one was required, he built two for symmetry' sake.)

Polk was such a visionary it took four decades before architects began implementing his wall-of-glass creation. When the Hallidie Building was in danger of being torn down, the American Institute of Architects (AIA) intervened, and now it's their chapter's San Francisco headquarters. The *New York Times* recently named it one of ten must-see buildings in the United States.

Polk was so hurt by the negative criticism that he never created another modern building, instead returning to his usual Neoclassical and Beaux-Art styles.

The building is named after Andrew Hallidie, inventor of the cable car.

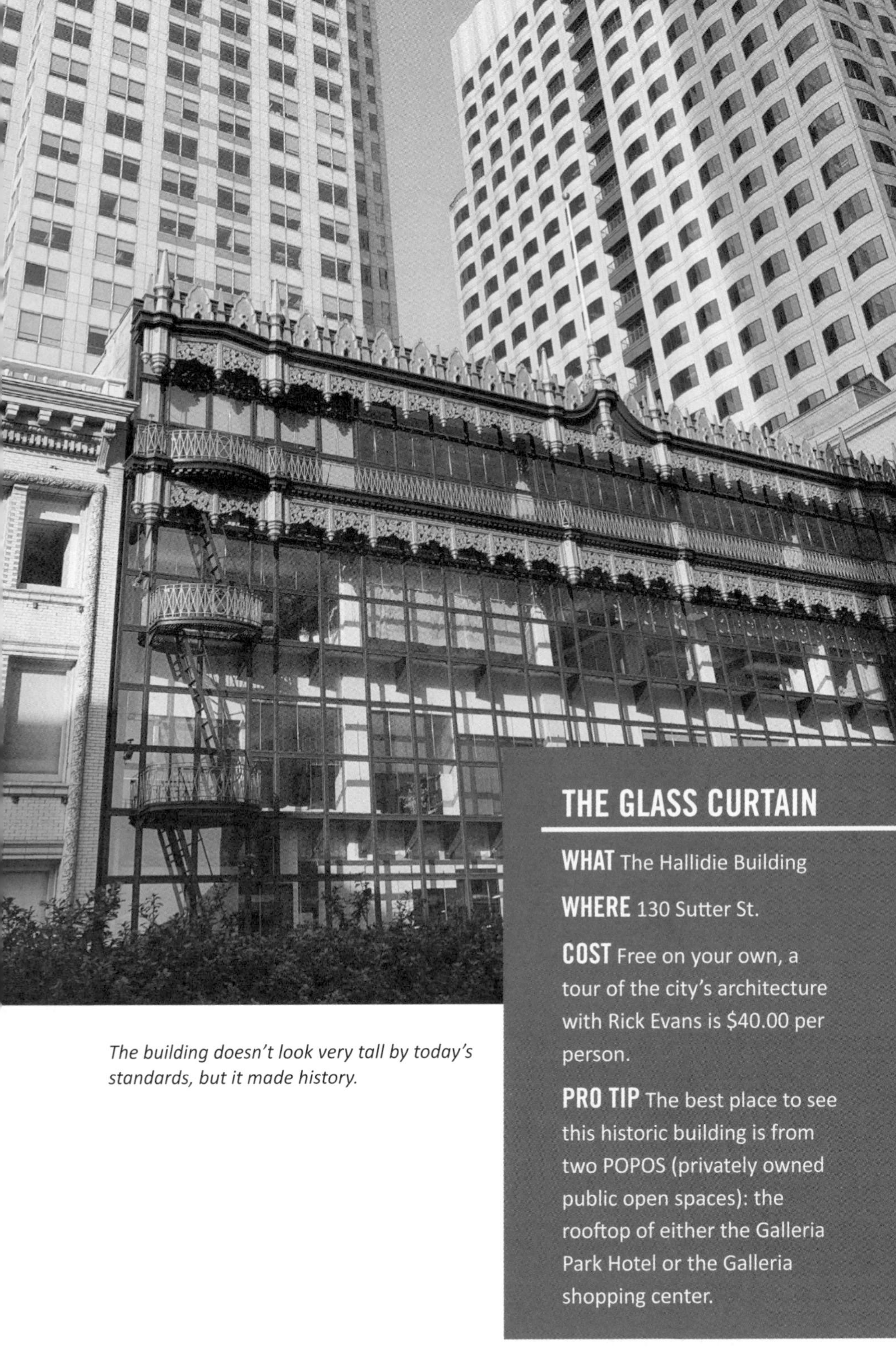

The building doesn't look very tall by today's standards, but it made history.

THE GLASS CURTAIN

WHAT The Hallidie Building

WHERE 130 Sutter St.

COST Free on your own, a tour of the city's architecture with Rick Evans is $40.00 per person.

PRO TIP The best place to see this historic building is from two POPOS (privately owned public open spaces): the rooftop of either the Galleria Park Hotel or the Galleria shopping center.

37 INSIDE ALCATRAZ

What are some tidbits you won't hear on the Alcatraz tour?

About 1.7 million people visit Alcatraz every year—zealous fans of the island are called Alcatrazophiles—but even they may not know everything. Here are a few lesser-known stories:

When it was a working prison, guards and prisoners claimed to have seen apparitions, including a pair of glowing red eyes peering into the darkness. Since then, non-profits—often Boy Scouts—have stayed overnight at Alcatraz, bravely sleeping in the tiny cells to test out the rumors of ghosts. The phantom jury is still out.

Before it was a federal prison Alcatraz was a fort and the tunnels built in case of enemy attack are still there.

The children of guards, who took the ferry to school in San Francisco, were forbidden to own toy guns in case the guards mistook them for the real thing.

Al Capone played the banjo in the prison's band, called the Rock Islanders.

In the early days inmates were only allowed to talk during mealtimes and recreation, but they somehow managed to communicate between cell grates.

Conversations between guests and inmates took place by an intercom monitored by guards. Forbidden topics included news of the outside world or conditions in the prison.

Every year the Dolphin Club holds an Escape from Alcatraz triathlon that includes swimming in the chilly Bay from Aquatic Park to the Island.

Be sure to make a reservation for the Alcatraz tour—it fills up quickly.

UNKNOWN ALCATRAZ

WHAT Obscure facts about Alcatraz

WHERE Alcatraz

COST Alcatraz daytime tickets: under $40.

PRO TIP Purchase a Behind-the-Scenes tour online to see things not included on the regular tour, such as underground caves used by the military.

Morton Sobell, author of *On Doing Time,* was infamous for helping Julius and Ethel Rosenberg, the alleged Communist spies who were executed in 1953.

When the prison closed in 1963, a Texas millionaire wanted to make it into a casino.

Native American activists, including actor Benjamin Bratt, occupied the island in 1969, demanding that the government cede the land. After the occupation ended in 1971, President Nixon ordered the demolition of the guard housing on the island to prevent any future occupations.

38 NATURE FRIENDS

Where is the hidden Austrian lodge?

San Franciscans escaping to Marin for their nature fix is nothing new. In 1912 a group of Germans and Austrians living in the city were hiking Mount Tamalpais when they stumbled upon a cabin. It was falling apart, but they only noticed the views of Mt. Tam's peak and the treetops of Muir Woods. It seemed the perfect place for a local chapter of Nature Friends, a European organization dating back to 1895, that offers a resting place for outdoor enthusiasts after a long day. They bought the shack and soon had more visitors than they could handle. In those days anyone who wanted to visit Mt. Tam (its affectionate nickname) had to endure a long journey from San Francisco involving a ferry, a train from Sausalito to Mill Valley, and then walking or taking the train up the mountain.

A few years later they demolished the cabin and built an Austrian–German alpine chalet on the site, complete with wooden balconies, carved ornamentation, and traditional folk paintings. This was not an easy feat in 1915 when the only way to haul in materials was by mule or on men's backs.

Nature Friends is a private club, but visitors are welcome on Sundays from 9 a.m. to 3 p.m. There's no restaurant, so pack your own refreshments, but there are board games and the occasional accordion player. The public is also invited to festivals in May, July, and September with folk dancing, live music, beer, and traditional food.

The Nature Friends Tourist Club welcomes new members and emphasizes that German–Austrian heritage is not necessary.

The Tourist Club holds several fundraisers—open to the public—for charities.

MT. TAM SURPRISE

WHAT An Austrian chalet, touristclubsf.org

WHERE Mt. Tam, reachable from the Redwood Trail or the Dipsea Trail to the Sun Trail. Parking lot is 30 Ridge Ave., Mill Valley, about a half mile from the Clubhouse.

COST Free to visit, the festivals have a fee.

PRO TIP Austrian restaurants, such as Leopold's, are the latest foodie trend in San Francisco.

39 EARTHQUAKE SHACKS

Did San Francisco invent the tiny house?

More than 100 years before the current craze for tiny houses, many San Franciscans were happily living in two-hundred-square-foot homes.

When the 1906 earthquake destroyed five hundred blocks and half the city, 250,000 people found themselves suddenly homeless. To deal with the crisis, the Army set up tent cities around town, in Washington Square Park, Dolores Park, Golden Gate Park, and the Presidio. When winter came the people still living in tents needed something warmer, so the Army collaborated with the city to build five thousand small wooden cottages, nicknamed "earthquake shacks."

Shacks were a misleading name for the high-end materials used: California redwood siding, fir floors, and a cedar roof. Painted green to blend in with the parks, the tiny houses were rent-to-own, another trend where San Francisco was ahead of its time. Tenants paid two dollars a month and when they reached fifty dollars, they owned it—with one catch. They were

LITTLE PLACES WITH BIG STORIES

WHAT Earthquake shacks

WHERE Presidio, Main Post, behind building 2

COST Free

PRO TIP If you want to find the ones scattered around the city, Outsidelands.org lists the location of all the remaining earthquake shacks.

Most people forgot about earthquake shacks until the 1980s when Jane F. Cryan lobbied to preserve them. Because of her efforts many shacks were preserved and others were declared city landmarks.

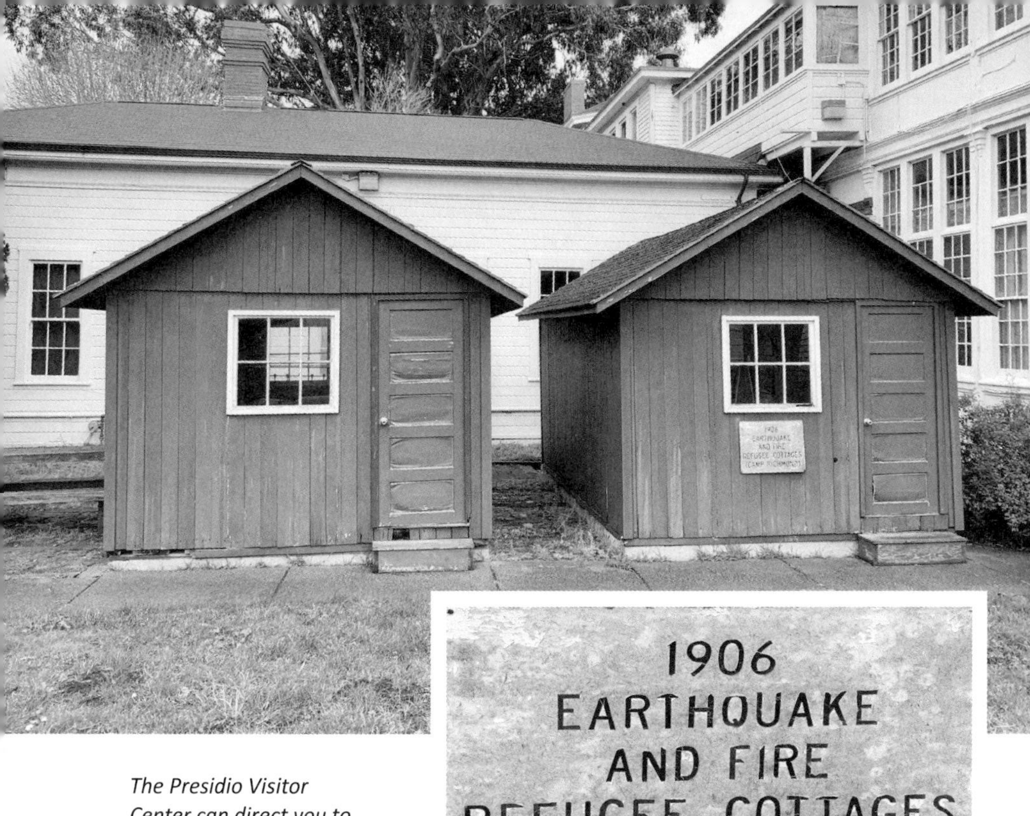

1906
EARTHQUAKE
AND FIRE
REFUGEE COTTAGES
(CAMP RICHMOND)

The Presidio Visitor Center can direct you to other hidden treasures in this park.

responsible for moving it, via horse and buggy, to a permanent location. For many it was the first home they owned.

There are still a small number of earthquake shacks around town, which sell for a minimum of a million dollars. Sometimes they're hard to spot because they've been remodeled and expanded or combined with another earthquake shack for more square footage.

40 FOGGY FRIEND

Who is Karl?

Every summer you see them, tourists in shorts and t-shirts shivering as they wait in long lines for a cable car ride. It's all Karl's fault, the locals' nickname for fog.

The moniker started with a Twitter account @Karlthefog. Created in 2010 by an anonymous tweeter it has more than 340 thousand followers. According to the *San Francisco Chronicle* the name refers to Karl in the movie *Big Fish*. Karl was a giant everyone was afraid of because they thought he would kill or eat them, when in fact he was just hungry and lonely. The handle is so well known it was a question on the TV show *Jeopardy*.

Karl comes to the city when it's sweltering in the East Bay; locals call it our natural air conditioning. It can be fifty-six degrees at Ocean Beach and just a half hour inland the highs will be in the 90s. Karl can be romantic, mysterious, and irritating. When he overstays his welcome residents call it a fogpocalypse.

Here on a sunny day? The Exploratorium has a fog bridge that will envelope you in mist and give you the true San Francisco experience.

Our summer begins in the fall. In September 2017, the city reached a record high of 106 degrees, says meteorologist Mike Pechner.

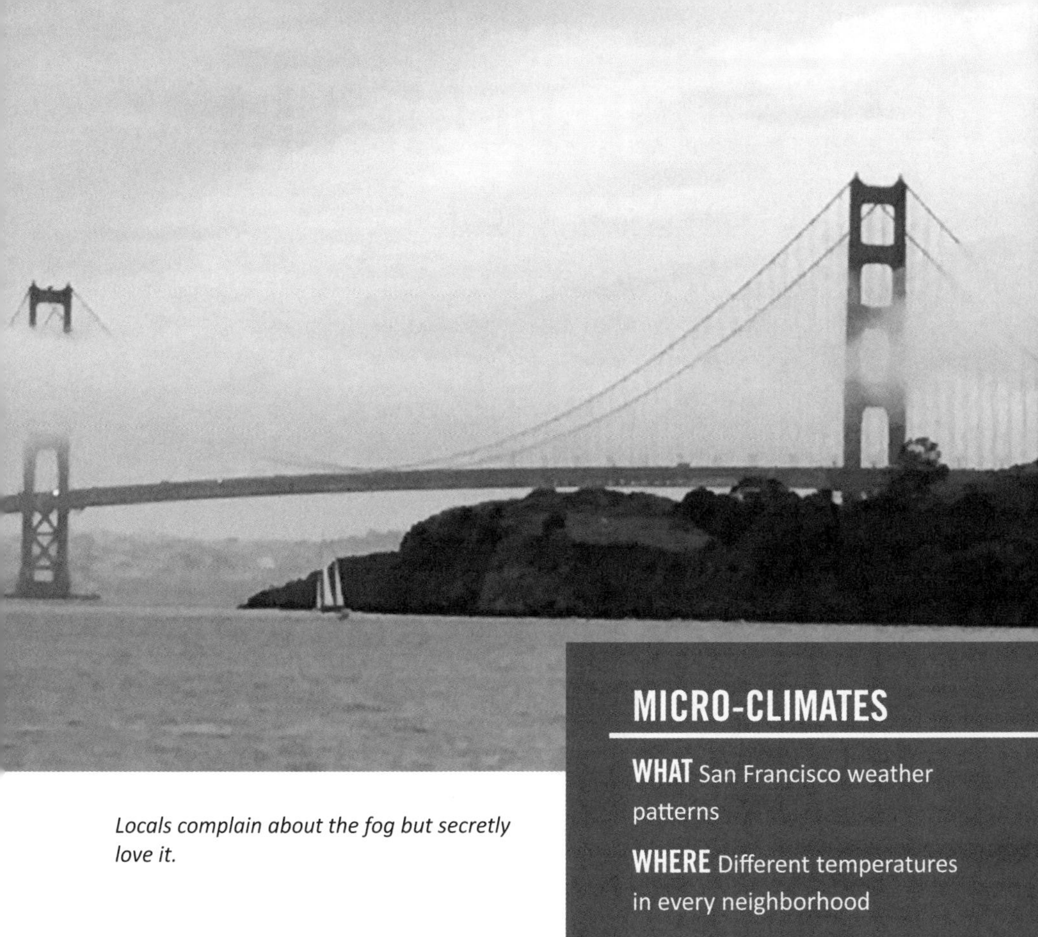

Locals complain about the fog but secretly love it.

MICRO-CLIMATES

WHAT San Francisco weather patterns

WHERE Different temperatures in every neighborhood

COST Free

PRO TIP Layering is key since the weather can change in a few blocks.

41 SF'S GOOD FORTUNE

Who invented the fortune cookie?

The origins of the fortune cookie have little to do with China and everything to do with San Francisco's role in world events.

It began in 1894 when the City built a Japanese Tea House for the California Midwinter International Exposition. Mr. Makoto Hagiwara made traditional Sembei cookies by hand for the café. He changed them slightly for the American sweet tooth, adding vanilla extract, but kept the traditional hidden prophecies.

His fortune changed when Japanese Americans were forced to move to internment camps during World War II. In their absence, Chinese bakers supplied the Tea House with their version of the fortune cookie. They were still handmade until the 1960s when San Franciscan Edward Louie invented the fortune cookie folding machine.

Over the years there has been debate over who invented the modern fortune cookie, but an SF court put that to rest. The Court of Historical Reviews and Appeals (a mock court) ruled that the city is the rightful "fortune cookie capital of the world."

Today the Golden Gate Fortune Cookie in Chinatown still makes fortune cookies by hand. You can sample the cookies, watch employees fold the dough, and take a photo—but it will cost you fifty cents!

The Japanese Tea Garden is the oldest public Japanese garden in the United States. They still offer fortune cookies although it's no longer a tradition in Japanese restaurants.

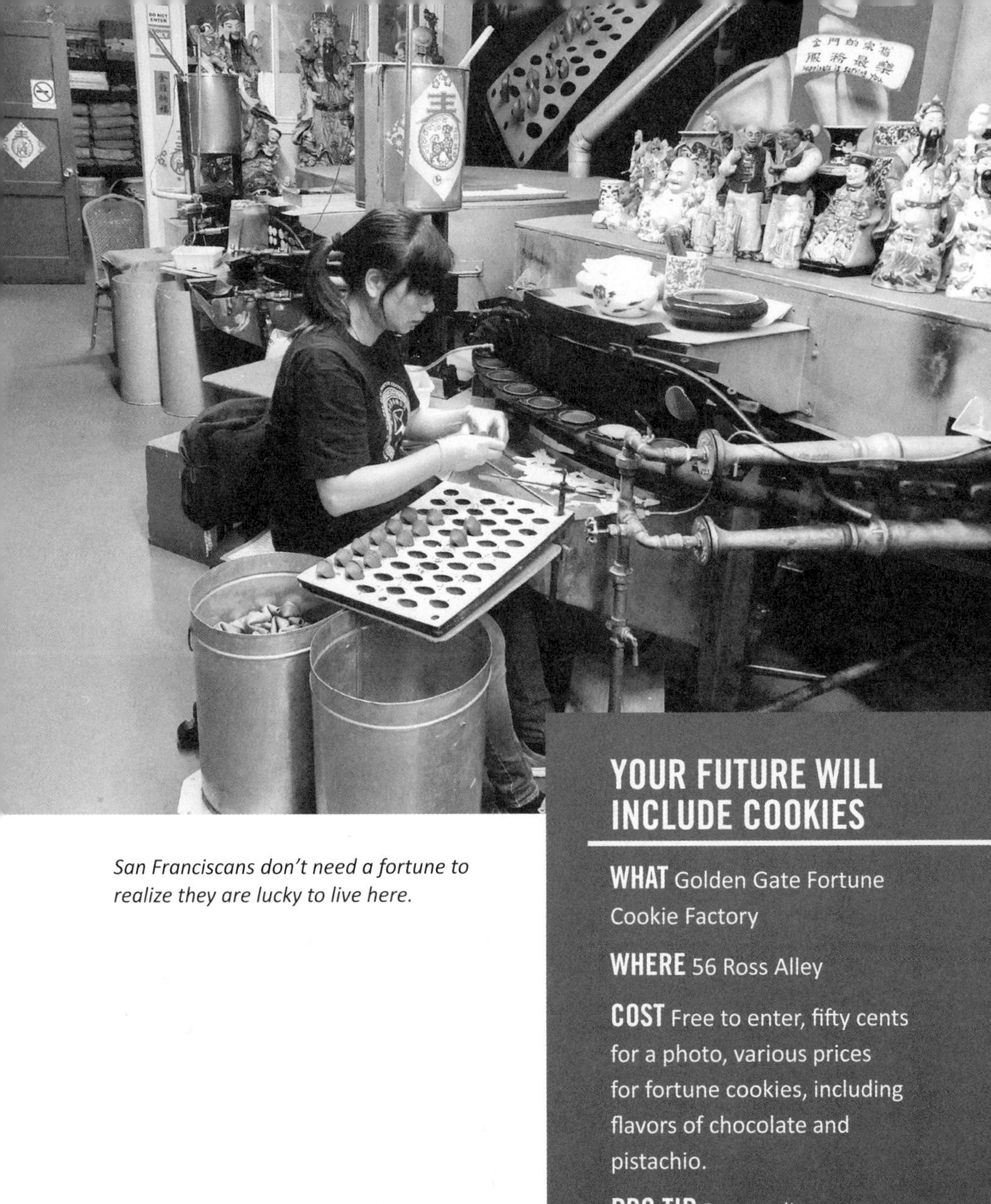

San Franciscans don't need a fortune to realize they are lucky to live here.

YOUR FUTURE WILL INCLUDE COOKIES

WHAT Golden Gate Fortune Cookie Factory

WHERE 56 Ross Alley

COST Free to enter, fifty cents for a photo, various prices for fortune cookies, including flavors of chocolate and pistachio.

PRO TIP Personalize your fortune cookies by writing your own messages.

42 OCEAN LINER HOUSE

Where can you see Humphrey Bogart?

If you're anxious to get your exercise while vacationing in San Francisco it's easy: just climb the steep Filbert Steps to Coit Tower. Along the way you'll hear the shrieking green parrots of Telegraph Hill, walk by cottages, hidden gardens, and one sleek building that will stop you in your tracks.

Jutting out over the Bay the curved white five-story building resembles a luxury cruise ship. In the Streamline Moderne Style, it was designed by architect Irvin Goldstine for the Malloch family. It's known as the Ocean Liner, the Malloch Building, or even just it's address, 1360 Montgomery Street.

Muralist Alfred DuPont used raised plaster to create three silver images—each forty-feet high—on the building's sides. These panels show a Spanish explorer holding a telescope to one eye, a worker standing above the Bay Bridge with planes above him and boats below, and a robed woman in front of a California map.

Film noir fans may recognize it from the movie *Dark Passage*. Lauran Bacall's character lived in apartment #10, and Humphrey Bogart recuperated from plastic surgery there after climbing the Filbert Steps. The current residents sometimes put a cutout of Bogie in the window.

The Streamline Moderne style copies the sleek curves of moving vehicles: trains, boats, planes and cars.

You can see another Art Moderne building on Treasure Island. Photo courtesy of John Williamson.

FILM HISTORY

WHAT Streamline Moderne style building

WHERE 1360 Montgomery St.

COST Free

PRO TIP Take the Greenwich Street steps on your way down the hill so you can see Julius Castle. Built in 1923, it's a Landmark building, formerly a restaurant.

43 STRANGE SAGA OF SAN FRANCISCO'S SONG

When was "I Left My Heart in San Francisco" a controversial song?

It seems hard to believe now but there was a time when many San Franciscans did not like Tony Bennett's love letter to the city. Two unknown composers wrote the tune in 1954 and it sat around for years until Tony Bennett discovered it. After an enthusiastic response at the Fairmont Hotel's Venetian Room Bennett recorded it on the B-side of a single that no one remembers. Luckily disc jockeys loved the San Francisco valentine and propelled it into a hit.

But not all San Franciscans loved the tune. In the 1980s Supervisor Quentin Kopp wanted to remove the tune as the city's official song and replace it with "San Francisco" from the 1936 movie by the same name starring Clark Gable and Jeannette McDonald.

Mayor Dianne Feinstein was vehemently opposed. The cable cars had just undergone a renovation for the Democratic National Convention, and Feinstein wanted Bennett riding

SAN FRANCISCO'S OFFICIAL BALLAD

WHAT Tony Bennett statue

WHERE Front of the Fairmont Hotel, 950 Mason St., Nob Hill

COST Free

PRO TIP While you're at the Fairmont get an umbrella drink at the Tonga Room, a tiki bar surrounding a lagoon (the hotel's old pool). Be sure to stick around for the tropical thunder and lightning.

"I left my Heart in San Francisco" is played every time the San Francisco Giants win a baseball game.

At age ninety Tony Bennett is still performing.

next to her, singing the popular tune for the politicians.

Newspaper columnists Herb Caen and Warren Hinkle supported Kopp and this inspired all 150 members of the Gay Men's Chorus to belt out "San Francisco" at City Hall. Some say the protest turned into a drunken brawl: it was enough to keep Bennett trapped in his hotel room, afraid of being booed.

Afterwards the city supervisors reached a compromise. The official song would be "San Francisco" and Bennett's tune would be the official ballad.

In 2016 the city embraced the heart he left behind in San Francisco and erected a statue of Bennett in front of the Fairmont. At the unveiling the crooner was happy to leave the hotel and greet an adoring crowd. In 2018 the song was added to the National Recording Registry by the Library of Congress for being "culturally, historically, or artistically significant."

POPOS (page 34)

COSTLY CABLE CARS (page 24)

MARITIME MUSEUM (page 18)

SLOWING DOWN TIME (page 46)

ART HOUSE (page 68)

FLOAT IN NORTH BEACH (page 10)

MURALS WITH A MESSAGE (page 42)

SECRET STAIRWAYS (page 36)

DUTCH TREAT (page 168)

LANDS END LABYRINTH (page 128)

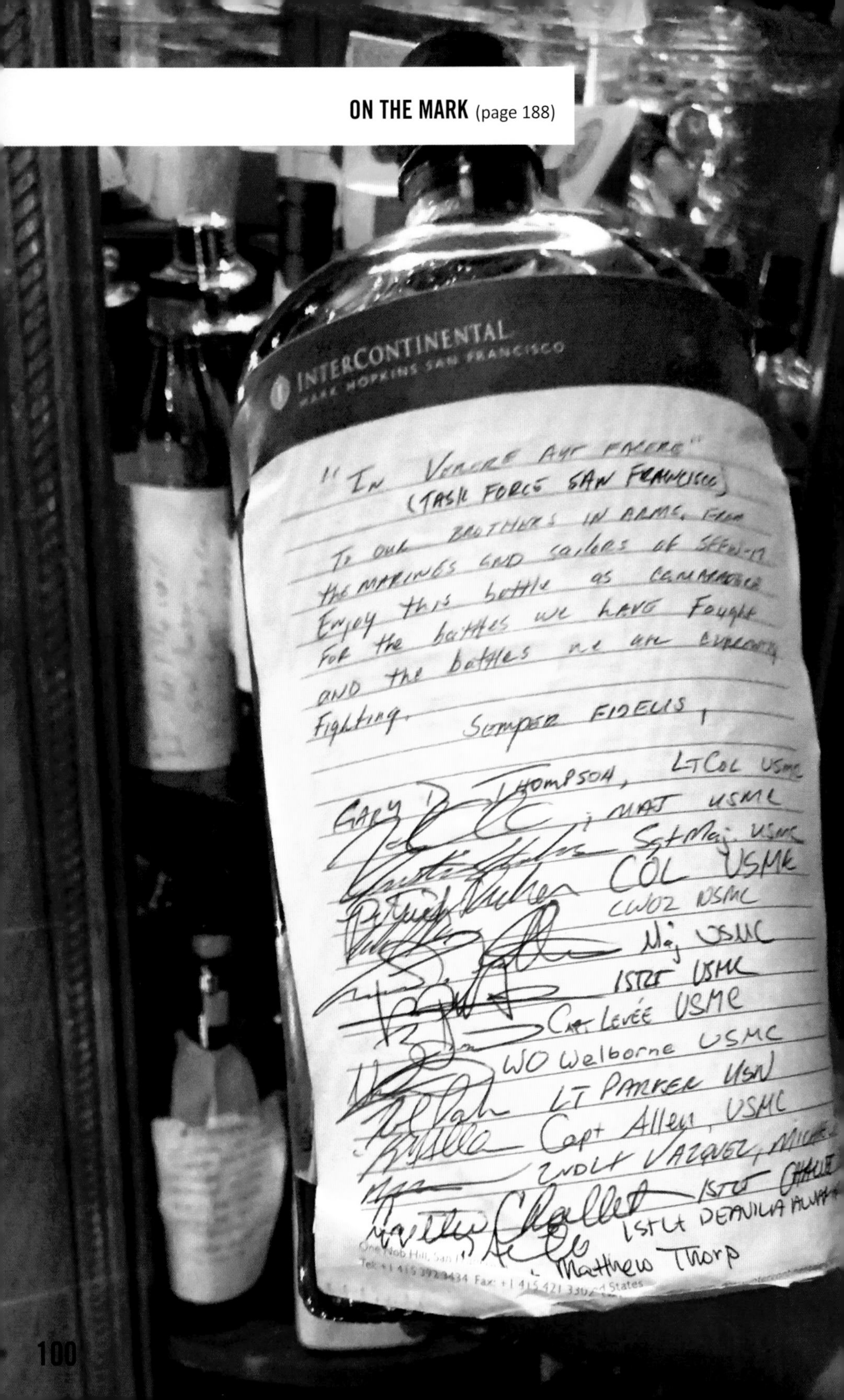
INTERCONTINENTAL
MARK HOPKINS SAN FRANCISCO
(TASK FORCE SAN FRANCISCO)
To our Brothers in Arms. From
the Marines and sailors of
Enjoy this bottle as
For the battles we have fought
and the battles we are
fighting. Semper Fidelis,
Gary Thompson, LtCol USMC
MAJ USMC
SgtMaj USMC
COL USMC
CWO2 USMC
Maj USMC
1stLt USMC
Capt Levée USMC
WO Welborne USMC
LT Parker USN
Capt Allen, USMC
2ndLt Vazquez,
1stLt
Matthew Thorp

FLOWER POWER (page 192)

NATIONAL LANDMARK (page 186)

SEA SQUATTERS (page 176)

BANK ON IT (page 144)

44 CHECKMATE

Where is the oldest continuously operating chess club in the United States?

It's trendy now to shop from "makers" but the city's affinity for locally made goods is not new . . . it began during the Gold Rush. In 1848 there were about 800 residents in San Francisco. Six years later the population exploded to 34,000, with 100,000 more arriving each year. Everything was imported and the city was desperate for local manufacturing and jobs for the miners who didn't strike gold.

So they copied an idea from Scotland and built a Mechanics' Institute (M.I.). The word *mechanic* then referred to anyone who created things . . . artisans, craftsmen, and inventors. M.I. taught technical classes, held social events to keep young men away from houses of ill repute, and—most important—gave members of the working class access to books.

Destroyed in the 1906 quake, it was rebuilt a few years later with Tennessee pink marble floors, Ionic columns, and a stunning spiral iron staircase. One of the oldest libraries on the west coast, its frequent visitors included John Muir, Domingo Ghirardelli, and Jack London, who was notorious for returning his books late.

It's not just a library; it's also home to the oldest continuously operating chess club in the United States. Bobby Fischer and Boris Spassky have both competed here. This world-renowned chess club holds frequent tournaments and offers free chess classes for grade school students and women.

In an effort to raise money in the early 1900s, the Institute held several fairs promoting locally made goods that paved the way for the Panama–Pacific Exposition in 1915.

The Mechanics Institute is trying to encourage more female chess players by offering free classes just for women.

THE ORIGINAL MAKERS

WHAT A private library in a landmark building with chess classes

WHERE 57 Post St.

COST Free for tours, individual membership is $120 a year.

PRO TIP Many of the events are open to the public including author readings, vintage movie screenings, and writing classes.

45 SHOOTOUT OVER SLAVERY

Where was the last notable duel in America?

You could say gold shined a bright light on slavery. In the late 1850s everyone wanted to strike it rich and that meant traveling to San Francisco, the gateway city to the Sierra Nevada. Many miners returned to the city or never left, settling instead in this boomtown.

The city was a mix of Free Soilers (abolitionists), Chivs (short for chivalry, the nickname Southern slave owners called themselves), slaves, and free African American settlers. This tense environment erupted into a deadly duel between two politicians who, some say, helped push the country into a civil war.

Despite their opposing views on slavery, David S. Terry, Chief Justice of the State Supreme Court, and Senator David Colbreth Broderick were pals . . . until the 1859 Democratic state convention.

Terry attacked Broderick for his anti-slavery views at the convention, and Broderick responded with insulting statements. When Terry lost his seat on the court, he blamed Broderick and challenged him to a duel. This was not unusual for Terry; he had previously stabbed another politician.

Fort Mason was a military post with a very limited Army presence, so it became home to a small but influential group of white residents openly hostile to slavery.

San Francisco had a pivotal role in ending slavery.

FREEDOM FIGHT

WHAT Haskell House

WHERE 3 Franklin St.

COST Free

PRO TIP There's also a Broderick statue in Fort Mason and a Broderick St. off Chestnut St. in the Marina District.

Duels were banned in San Francisco, so they moved the shootout to Lake Merced, located just south of the city at that time and now part of San Francisco. Broderick was unfamiliar with his gun and it misfired, whereas Terry, who had been practicing with the same gun, shot Broderick in the chest. Broderick died three days later, his last words reportedly, "They killed me because I am opposed to the extension of slavery and the corruption of justice." He died in the home of his friend Leonidas Haskell, a Free-Soiler who was also politically connected.

46 HOW THE BAY WAS SAVED

Why is a warehouse filled with a huge model of the Bay?

Along the far end of the Sausalito waterfront, away from downtown and the tourists who bicycle over the Golden Gate Bridge, there's a World War II era warehouse with a 3-D display of the San Francisco Bay and the Sacramento Delta.

The working hydraulic model is spread out over an acre and a half in a warehouse that was once part of Marinship, a World War II era shipyard. Seeing the waterways spread at your feet is an astonishing site and even more impressive when you learn it saved the San Francisco Bay.

In the 1950s an actor named John Reber came up with the idea of damning the Bay to form freshwater lakes. Reber's showman skills won over a lot of converts, especially farmers who saw the benefit of more water for crops.

Congress took the Reber Plan so seriously it gave the US Army Corps of Engineers millions to investigate its feasibility. The Army created the Bay Model to simulate the regions' watersheds in various conditions, including saltwater, flooding, oil spills, and frequent tidal changes. Tests indicated the Reber Plan was a disastrous idea and the Bay was saved.

THE BAY AT YOUR FEET

WHAT Bay Model Visitors Center

WHERE 2100 Bridgeway Sausalito; the entrance is on the water.

COST Free

PRO TIP For lunch or dinner, walk to the nearby Le Garage restaurant. Located in a warehouse facing the harbor, this casual bistro is owned by two Frenchmen who encourage you to relax and take your time.

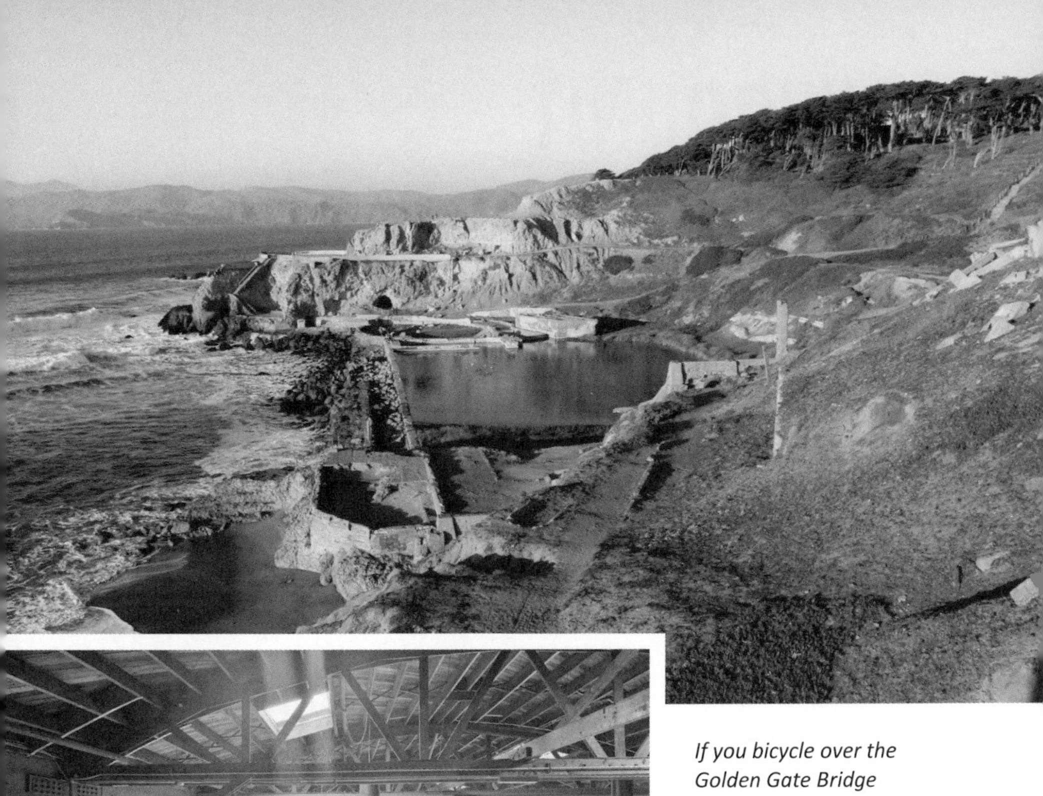

If you bicycle over the Golden Gate Bridge keep going to reach the Bay Model. Top picture courtesy of John Williamson.

Today computers are a more reliable way to study the waterways but the Army keeps the Bay Model as a museum and an educational tool. The Bay Model environmental tour is a popular field trip for Bay Area schools.

Protecting the Bay is a continual concern. SavetheBay.org is dedicated to preserving and restoring the Bay from pollution and climate change.

47 WHODUNIT

Where did Dashiell Hammet get his inspiration for *The Maltese Falcon*?

So, it's like this, see—I was writing ad copy for Samuel's Jewelry, and this redheaded broad walks in—a real tomato. A lot of folks say she was the inspiration for Brigid O'Shaughnessy, that no-good temptress in *The Maltese Falcon*. You won't find out from me. I'm no squealer—just ask Joe McCarthy.

In the Roaring '20s I got a lot of ideas in San Francisco. Guess you could say that's where I made it big. *The Falcon* is set in the city, and boy are they proud of that. There's even a restaurant all about me—John's Grill. It has a plaque outside . . . says I wrote the book there but don't believe it, kid. I typed it in my apartment at 891 Post Street, clicking away every day after shoving my Murphy bed back in the wall. Take a tour with Don Herron—he's a straight shooter. He'll tell you John's Grill is the place Sam Archer ordered chops, baked potatoes, and sliced tomatoes for lunch and that's still on the menu—can you beat that? There's a replica of the Maltese Falcon upstairs and it's been stolen twice. Didn't they learn anything from my novel?

Funny thing. Burritt Street, where Brigid iced my partner Miles Archer? They put up a plaque to commemorate this fake

---

The Dashiell Hammett Tour is the oldest literary walking tour in the country.

When Dashiell Hammett's daughter went on the walking tour, she said the correct pronunciation of his name was Dash-eel.

LITERARY LEGACY

WHAT Dashiell Hammett Tour
www.donherron.com

WHERE Meet at the James Flood Building

COST $20.00

PRO TIP Wear comfy shoes, as you'll walk up and down a lot of hills.

murder. There's also a Dashiell Hammett Street, a tiny alley, but what the heck—I like things gritty.

People believed my stories because I was a private eye at the Pinkerton Detective Agency in the James Flood Building before I worked at Shreves. Directors tried making *The Maltese Falcon* into a movie—twice—but they bombed. Then they wised up and cast Humphrey Bogart. It made Bogie's career and mine. Maybe you heard of a little movie I made after that called *The Thin Man*.

48 BEAT GOES ON . . .

Why was San Francisco the heart of the beat movement?

In the 1950s Vesuvio Café sold beatnik kits. Each provided everything a square needed to be a cool daddy-o: black-rimmed eyeglasses, a beret, sandals, and a turtleneck. Ironic when you consider the Beat Generation opposed conformity. *San Francisco Chronicle* columnist Herb Caen is credited with creating the word *beatnik*. Sputnik had just launched and he combined the two words, leading many to believe the Beats were communists.

In the uptight '50s beats flocked to hip and tolerant San Francisco. Jack Kerouac coined the term Beat Generation, denoting that they were tired.

Followers, including Allen Ginsberg, William S. Burroughs, and Maya Angelou, espoused their philosophy in the cafés and bars of bohemian North Beach. Vesuvio Café kept Jack Kerouac from meeting author Henry Miller. In 1960, Miller invited Kerouac to Big Sur and Kerouac had a drink for the road but he didn't stop at one. Every hour Kerouac phoned Miller and said he'd be there soon

THE ORIGINAL HIPSTERS

WHAT The only museum dedicated to the Beat Generation

WHERE 540 Broadway St.

COST $8.00

PRO TIP The Beat Museum is undergoing a seismic retrofit in 2019 so check to see if it is open.

Lawrence Ferlinghetti discovered the writers. At age one hundred he's owner of City Lights, the first all paperback bookstore in the country.

Hipsters are nothing new . . . beatniks started the movement.

. . . until they both gave up. When Bob Dylan visited Vesuvio he ordered tea, influencing the Beats to follow suit, according to Janet Clyde, an owner of the bar. In the mornings the Beats hung out at Café Trieste, the first espresso café on the West Coast. Popular lore says they wrote many of their best-selling books here.

Kerouac composed much of *On The Road* at 29 Russell Street in Russian Hill, the house he shared with Neal Cassady, who was the inspiration for Dean Moriarty in the novel. When the Beats were phased out by hippies, Cassady went along for the ride, driving the Merry Prankster bus. You can find out more about this interesting time in San Francisco at the Beat Museum, the only one of its kind in the world.

49 SECRET GARDEN

Where can you find farmers in the city?

Nestled among the historic buildings at Fort Mason, there's a sunny spot high above the Bay where locals pay to dig in the dirt. This community garden is so popular it has a waiting list eight years long.

"It's an oasis in the middle of the city," says Bernadette Festa, who grows artichokes, kale, and strawberries. "I love being close to the soil in a tranquil setting. The best part is the satisfaction from eating the fresh fruit and vegetables that I grew."

COUNTRY IN THE CITY

WHAT Fort Mason Community Garden

WHERE Pope Road, Fort Mason

COST Free to browse; annual dues for members is $100

PRO TIP Walk from the garden to Greens vegetarian restaurant, a pioneer in using organic produce.

Surprisingly, these gardeners have the San Francisco Arts Commission (SFAC) to thank for their little plot of land in the middle of the city. In the 1970s SFAC leaders, including famed artist Ruth Asawa, wanted to educate students on the origins of their food. (What this has to do with art is a mystery—perhaps the art of eating?) At the same time Galileo High School moved many classes into empty barracks at Fort Mason so it made sense to locate a school/community garden in the Great Meadow.

At one point, Fort Mason wanted to move the garden to the foot of Laguna Street, but horticulturalists protested over the traffic, car fumes, and noise. Instead gardeners suggested moving it behind the Administration building. Officials were worried about the nearby historic buildings dating back to

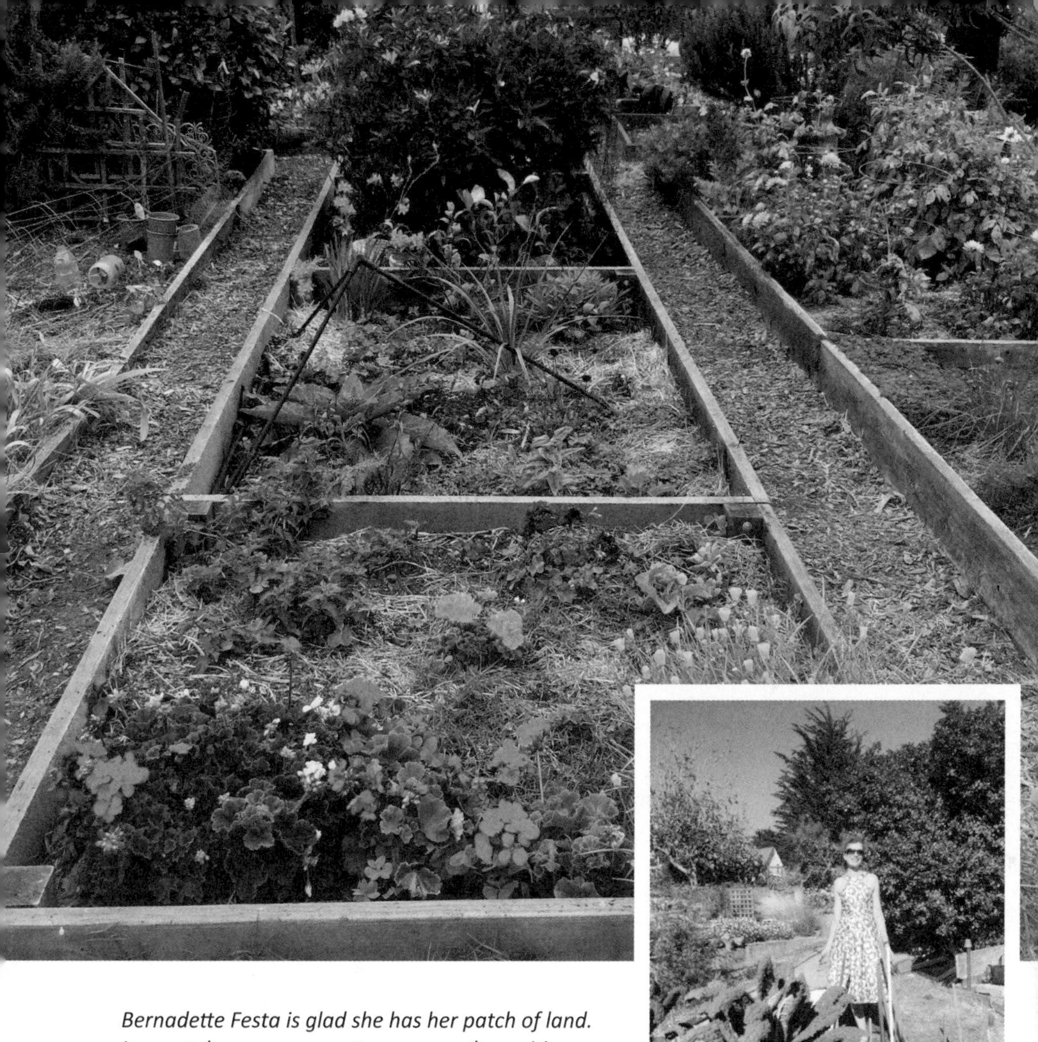

Bernadette Festa is glad she has her patch of land. It now takes many years to move up the waiting list. The waiting list is long to get your patch of land at this community garden. Top photo courtesy of Judith Calson.

the Civil War, but when research revealed this location was the original garden for the military, the brass had to say yes.

Today there are 125 garden plots, each twenty-by-five feet, and no pesticides are allowed.

The garden is also a popular spot for bird lovers.

50 WATERWORKS

What are those red brick circles on streets all over town?

There are concrete vaults in the city that contain something more valuable than money or jewels—water. From droughts to devastating fires, lack of H_2O has always been a problem for the city.

In the 1800s the city had six major fires, and even though the ocean and the Bay surround San Francisco, it was impossible to get the water inland. To avoid any more of these catastrophes, the city built underground cisterns that are marked with a circle of red bricks embedded in the street.

In 1906 the earthquake severed water lines, and in the fires that followed, five hundred city blocks were destroyed over three days. The cisterns were one of the few sources of water available, and they're credited with saving Telegraph Hill.

Naturally when the city was rebuilt one of their top priorities was creating an auxiliary water supply system. It included fireboats, pump stations with tunnels that suck in water from the Bay, and a dramatic increase in the number of cisterns. The largest one is located at Civic Center near City Hall. In 2010 voters approved an earthquake safety bond measure to maintain and upgrade the firefighting water system.

San Francisco is the only city that has these underground artificial lakes.

San Francisco is one of the few cities with fireboats.

EMERGENCY H_2O

WHAT Red brick circles on San Francisco streets

WHERE Located throughout the city

COST Free

PRO TIP If you want to follow the red brick road, outsidelands.org has a map.

51 MODEL CLUB

What's the oldest yacht club in San Francisco?

It's not what you'd expect. It's a tiny club filled with even smaller boats: sailboats, powerboats, a raft filled with Barbie dolls (more on that later), and even steamboats.

The Model Yacht Club is home to one of the world's largest collections of scale model boats, most of them built by members. Boats range from two and a half feet to nearly eight feet long. Formed in 1898, it's the oldest continuously operating yacht club of its kind in the nation, according to Vice Commodore Rob Weaver. It's also the smallest and oldest yacht club in San Francisco.

Although these boats look like toys, the skippers are as competitive as America's Cup captains. Weaver says members are continually experimenting with new radio-controlled gadgets and tweaking masts and rigs to increase their speed on Spreckles Lake. Whatever they're doing is working; the Club holds the international record for model boat regatta championships. "Boaters range in age from eight to eighty-eight," says Weaver, "and we're always looking for new members."

About that Barbie raft . . . it's for a good cause. Members surround it with foam icebergs to practice rescue operations.

THE RACE IS ON

WHAT Model Yacht Club

WHERE Spreckles Lake, Golden Gate Park, 36th Ave. and Fulton St. entrance

COST Free

PRO TIP The public is welcome to visit the Clubhouse anytime it's open, usually weekends during races.

Skippers are just as competitive with these model boat races as America's Cup captains.

Be sure to check out the three steamboats and the gas-powered cabin cruiser on display in glass cases.

52 CITY GUIDES

Who offers free walking tours of San Francisco?

The Summer of Love, a Ghost Walk, Silent Movie locations . . . these are just a few of the free tours you can take every day in San Francisco. They're offered by City Guides, a non-profit organization with more than three hundred volunteers, sponsored by the San Francisco Public Library.

"Other cities have tours but they usually charge a fee; we believe we're the only free volunteer tour organization in the country," says Jef Friedel, program manager. It was the brainchild of Gladys Hansen, a San Francisco city archivist who died in 2017. After numerous requests from the mayor's office for VIP tours of City Hall and the Civic Center, she saw a need for trained docents. She wrote scripts for the tour guides that included interesting and humorous factoids because she thought history should be fun.

She didn't have a degree and when her boss suggested she go back to school so she could be promoted, it backfired. The professors informed the library managers she didn't need further education—they came to *her* for information! She's best known for her groundbreaking research on the 1906 earthquake. In her book *Denial of Disaster*, she concludes the death toll was much higher than the 478 listed at the time, and closer to 4,000.

The City Guides volunteers undergo rigorous training and lead tours fifty-two weeks a year, rain or shine. Some of the most popular tours include: Fisherman's Wharf and

---

No need to make a reservation, just show up at the location on the website: www.cityguides.org.

San Francisco has so many stories there are multiple daily tours. The Palace of Fine Arts is a popular one. Photo courtesy of John Williamson.

Chinatown, and the more unusual tours include Alfred Hitchcock's San Francisco, Billionaires Row, Art Deco in the Marina, and North Beach at Night.

WALKING TOURS

WHAT City Guides

WHERE San Francisco, from Ocean Beach to North Beach

COST Free, but they do ask for donations to help keep the program going.

PRO TIP A few of the tours require a reservation such as the Diego Rivera mural in the Stock Exchange tower and the Fairmont hotel.

53 MR. SAN FRANCISCO

Who wrote the longest running newspaper column in the country?

Back when people read a print newspaper every morning, there was one column nobody missed: Herb Caen.

A transplant from Sacramento—although he claimed his parents conceived him in San Francisco—he lovingly wrote about the people, places, and trends of the City by the Bay. In this era of social media it's difficult to understand the impact of his six-day-a-week column in the *San Francisco Chronicle* which he pounded out with two fingers on a Royal typewriter 'til the end.

If he recommended a restaurant or store it had instant cachet. He mingled with socialites but also covered the downtrodden. He won a special Pulitzer Prize for being the voice and conscience of a city.

Caen is credited with coining the words beatnik, Bersekely (for Berkeley), and Baghdad by the Bay (also the title of one of his books). His role model was Walter Winchell and in his suit and fedora, frequently holding a martini, Caen seemed to be from a bygone era. Before *People* magazine, he was gossiping about the high society set and politicians' scandals. His best friends were Mayor Willie Brown and Wilkes Bashford, former

---

Caen wrote a book called *Don't Call it Frisco* and, as with everything he advised, San Franciscans listened.

Herb Caen lives on thanks to the Twitter account @HerbCaenDaily.

THE CAEN HANG OUT

WHAT Le Central

WHERE 453 Bush St.

COST It can be pricey but Happy Hour is a good deal.

PRO TIP Happy Hour, with mussells, truffle fries and burgers, starts at 2 p.m.

owner of an exclusive clothing store by the same name. The trio had a standing date for lunch at Le Central, a Parisian restaurant downtown. He died in 1997 at the age of 80, and in his honor there's a Herb Caen Way along the Embarcadero and a streetcar named after him.

54 STINKY SATURDAYS

What happens to our poo?

It's the hottest ticket in town—booked months in advance. It's not a chance to see *Hamilton* or a Warriors game; it's the city's underground! Each month people excitedly sign up for free tours of San Francisco's sewer system or as the city markets it: Wastewater Treatment Plants.

I went to the Southeast Treatment Plant, which handles 80 percent of San Francisco's sewage. There is another treatment plant near the zoo, called Oceanside. Both plants are undergoing long-needed renovations; parts of the City's sewer system date back to the Gold Rush. Like most special events it requires a dress code, in this case: closed-toe shoes, long-sleeve shirt and long pants, a hard hat, reflective vest, and optional latex gloves.

Our tour guide was a lawyer who said he quit and went to work for the wastewater plant because he wants to make a difference. He's proud that the city's sewers go above and beyond strict environmental laws.

San Francisco has a rare sewage system that's combined; the system collects and treats storm water and whatever comes from showers and toilets. Workers have to handle anything that comes down the pipes, from wedding rings to money to a family of ducks—still alive!

Cleaning up human waste starts with removing excess water. Forgive me if this puts you off sweets but the factory

---

Anybody who works or lives in San Francisco can "adopt a drain" at: adoptadrain.sfwater.org. The City gives you the tools to keep your drain clean.

The Public Utilities Commission also has tours of their new green building.

SEWER SECRETS

WHAT Touring the Southeast Wastewater Treatment Plant

WHERE 750 Phelps St.

COST Free

PRO TIP This plant is hidden in a remote neighborhood that most residents are not even aware of, so it's easiest to reach by car (with GPS).

belt for sludge resembles a taffy-pulling machine. It works like a cow's digestive system, producing methane gas that's used for electricity and hot water and after the bacteria is removed farmers use it as fertilizer to improve their soil.

The tour ends with the opportunity to touch and smell the end product that had the aroma of . . . nothing. In fact, although I called it Stinky Saturday, the plant was remarkably odor free. I'm told the Oceanside plant tour is more fragrant.

55 BEST PLACE TO GET LOST

Why is there a circle of rocks on the edge of the Lands End trail?

Under cover of night with only the stars to guide him Eduardo Aguilera picked up rocks from Ocean beach, climbed up a steep dirt path, and quietly laid his stones in a pattern on the cliff top. He worked after sundown to avoid the Park Rangers whom he feared would not support his dream of creating a labyrinth on the edge of the world, Lands End.

A PBS program on the Chartres, France labyrinth inspired him. "Building it felt like I was connecting to ancient cultures," says Aguilera.

Since 2004 hundreds have enjoyed his creation except when vandals threw the rocks into the crashing waves below. When Eduardo was too busy at his auto detailing business to recreate his path Colleen Yerge came to the rescue, earning her nickname, "The Labyrinth Keeper." The last time the artwork was destroyed she reached out through social media and two hundred volunteers showed up.

"I didn't even know what a labyrinth was until I discovered his," says Yerge. "It was a spiritual awakening for me. It's the most beautiful place in all of San Francisco. The weather changes all the time: it can be windy or foggy and then the sun

---

***Smithsonian* magazine calls it among the top ten labyrinths in the world.**

Take your time finding your way out—the view is incredible. Photo courtesy of John Williamson.

comes out and you see dolphins dancing in the waves below. It's quite a gift Eduardo has given us."

As for those Park Rangers, today they gladly direct tourists to the site.

SPIRITUAL SPOT

WHAT Lands End Labyrinth

WHERE End of Lands End Trail

COST Free

PRO TIP Wear hiking boots. The path to the Labyrinth is rocky and steep.

56 ROYAL ACCOMMODATIONS

What Hotel has a Rich history?

San Francisco and drama are intertwined and the Palace Hotel has seen it all. In 1875 it was called the largest and most costly hotel in the world. It boasted hydraulic elevators lined in redwood called "rising rooms."

The hotel was gutted by the fires following the 1906 quake. Ironically the city tapped into the hotel's sub basements water source and by the time the fires reached the hotel the water was gone, says Renee Roberts, spokesperson for the Palace Hotel.

Rebuilt in 1909 the hotel unveiled stained glass, Austrian crystal chandeliers, and The Garden Court (also known as the Palm Court). The elegant restaurant is San Francisco's only interior landmark.

Instead of using washers to suspend the glass panels from cables in the Garden Court, the architect found pennies were the perfect weight and size. There are about 150 "pennies from heaven" supporting the interior glass ceiling.

RETRO GLAMOUR

WHAT The Palace Hotel

WHERE 2 New Montgomery St.

COST Varies

PRO TIP The Garden Court is famous for its Sunday brunch and high tea.

A former Palace bartender William Boothbe is called the first mixologist.

Children staying at The Palace Hotel can take part in a treasure hunt where they locate historical items. Top photo courtesy of John Williamson, left photo courtesy of Palace Hotel.

As part of their grand re-opening the Palace commissioned Maxfield Parrish for an original piece of art. Parrish painted himself as the Pied Piper leading people out of Hamelin Germany, and in the background you see his wife, two sons, and his mistress! It's on display in the Pied Piper bar.

One of the hotel's resident artists began as a dishwasher. In the 1920s, management noticed Antonio Sotomayor's caricatures of the wait staff and hired him as the in-house artist. He went on to draw San Francisco celebrities, and you can see his caricatures in the Pied Piper bar.

57 DOG HEAVEN

What is the Presidio Pet Cemetery?

It's common knowledge that those who served in the military are often buried in a veterans cemetery but did you know that in San Francisco their four-legged friends are nearby?

At the Presidio Pet Cemetery, Fido and Fluffy are resting in peace in a graveyard with million-dollar views. A white picket fence and a dozen Monterey pine trees surround the graveyard of pets adored and respected by enlisted men and women and their families. There are handmade headstones for dogs, cats, parakeets, lizards, goldfish and even mice. "The love these animals gave will never be forgotten," reads one moving epitaph.

No one is sure how the cemetery got started, but according to one legend it was a burial ground for hardworking, loyal cavalry horses in the 19th century. Another anecdote claims that the military-trained WWII K9 Corps dogs were the first to be buried here. The oldest markers date to the 1950s when the Presidio was under the control of Lt. General Joseph M. Swing, and some believe he authorized the cemetery.

A RESTING PLACE FOR MAN'S BEST FRIEND

WHAT Presidio Pet Cemetery

WHERE McDowell Ave. at Crissy Field

COST Free

PRO TIP While you're at the Presidio check out the lobby of Lucasfilm, Ltd. It has a full-size 6'6" Darth Vader and a built-to-scale Yoda is standing guard outside.

The cemetery is now closed to further interments, and the non-profit group Sword to Plowshares maintains the site.

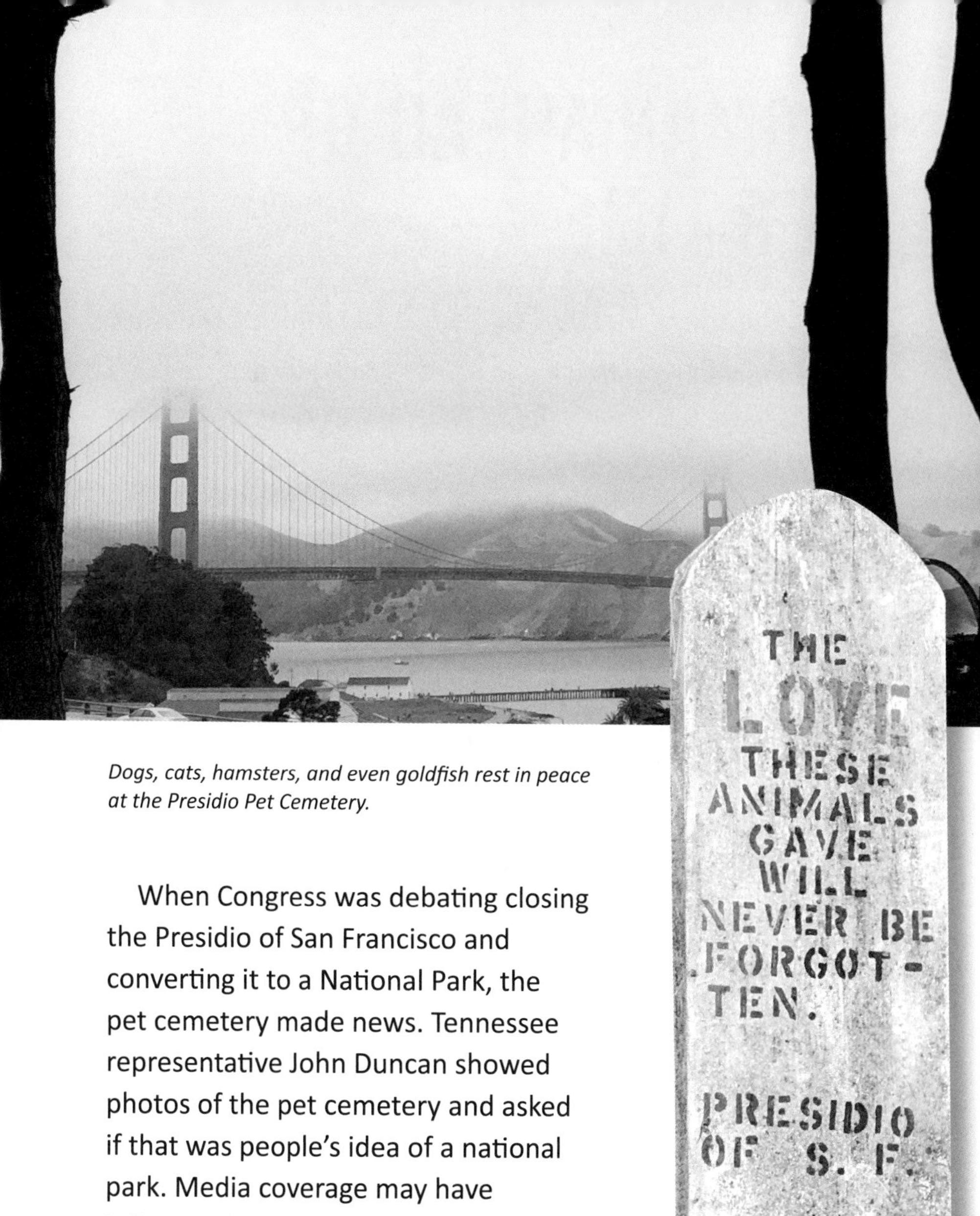

Dogs, cats, hamsters, and even goldfish rest in peace at the Presidio Pet Cemetery.

When Congress was debating closing the Presidio of San Francisco and converting it to a National Park, the pet cemetery made news. Tennessee representative John Duncan showed photos of the pet cemetery and asked if that was people's idea of a national park. Media coverage may have influenced Congress to create a unique arrangement within the National Park System: the Presidio Trust. This quasi-government agency manages the Presidio as a self-sustaining park without taxpayer support in collaboration with the National Park Service and the private Golden Gate National Parks Conservancy.

58 WOMAN AHEAD OF HER TIME

Who is the memorialized by the city's smallest park?

If someone made a movie about Mary Ellen Pleasant no one would believe it. She was a freed slave who became one of the richest women in America.

Historians believe she was originally a slave from the South who moved to the East Coast after she was freed where she became active in the Underground Railroad. When the Fugitive Slave Act passed in 1850 allowing slave owners to come north and retrieve their escaped slaves with the help of law enforcement, Pleasant's abolitionist leanings made her a target. She escaped to San Francisco where she found a more welcoming environment.

There were bachelors waiting at the dock for Pleasant to disembark because word of her amazing cooking had spread through town. After a bidding war for her culinary services she turned them all down and opened her own restaurant with money her deceased husband left her. Her restaurant was a favorite of wealthy men, and she instructed the servers to listen carefully and report back any investment tips. A shrewd businesswoman she owned apartment buildings, laundries, and a boardinghouse.

One day when a conductor refused to let her board a streetcar, Pleasant sued the transportation company and won, one hundred years before Rosa Parks.

On the corner of Octavia and Bush there's a plaque for Pleasant that says she was an entrepreneur, civil rights activist, and a friend of John Brown.

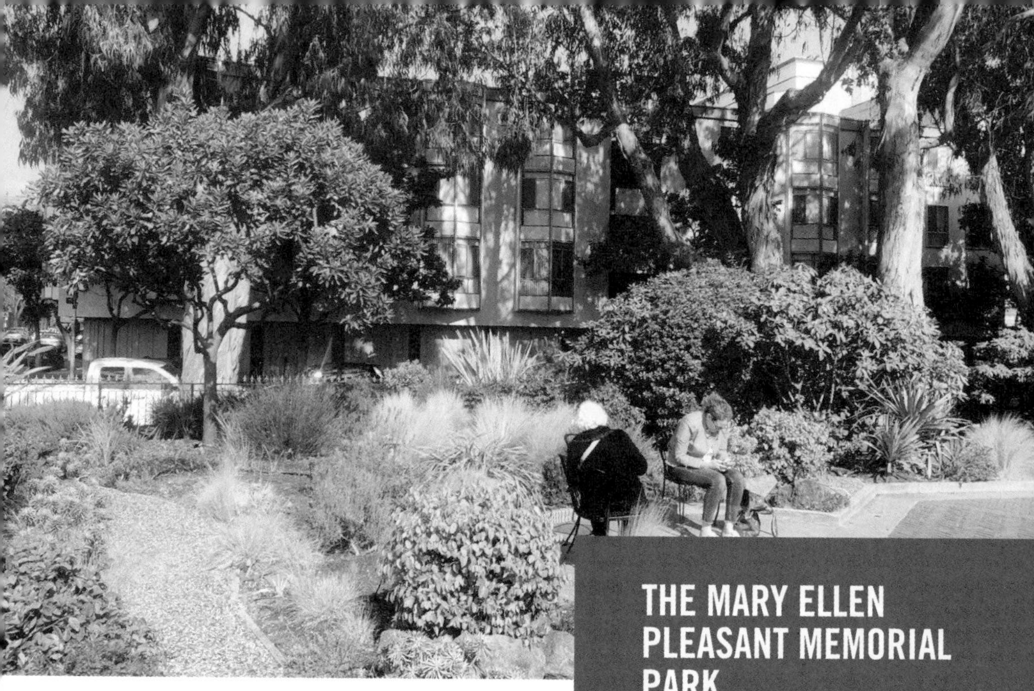

She was the Oprah of her time.

THE MARY ELLEN PLEASANT MEMORIAL PARK

WHAT A street lined with Eucalyptus trees planted by Mary Ellen Pleasant

WHERE Octavia St. at Bush

COST Free

PRO TIP The Healing Arts Center at Bush and Octavia is where Pleasant's mansion and stables once stood, running from Bush to Sutter.

Rumor has it she fell in love with Thomas Bell, a white man, and he moved into her thirty-room mansion—with his wife. Pleasant reportedly took a page out of Prince Charles' and Camilla's book and found the woman for Bell to marry. Because Pleasant was African American, Bell had to conduct all of her financial transactions.

Bell died after falling down the stairs and although a court said it was an accident, many blamed Pleasant. After the newspaper printed an article in 1899 about Pleasant, she and Bell's widow had a screaming fight and Pleasant left—for good.

The Mary Ellen Pleasant Memorial Park, a National Landmark, is six enormous eucalyptus gum trees (out of the original twenty she planted) on Octavia Street, where her mansion was located.

59 CRITICAL MASS

Why do bicyclists gather once a month on Market Street?

At 5:30 p.m. on the last Friday of each month hundreds of bikers congregate at Justin (Pee Wee) Herman Plaza, as locals call it, to join Critical Mass. It's a bicycle ride through the City and the purpose depends on whom you ask. It's a celebration, an alternative transportation promotion, or a way to make motorists aware of bicyclists on the road.

It can be whatever you want it to be because there's no one in charge of Critical Mass. Chris Carlsson, one of the founders, calls it xeroxcracy . . . meaning bikers are encouraged to make posters, buttons and mother make posters, buttons and other materials to promote the rides.

It's not surprising that Critical Mass started here since SF had the first bike club on the West Coast in 1876, second in the nation. In the 1890s bikes were a new and inexpensive form of transportation and there were reportedly two bikes for every fifteen people. Originally city leaders only allowed bikers to ride early in the morning in Golden Gate Park.

Women loved the freedom of bikes; they could go outside unchaperoned wearing bloomers. In 1896 Margaret Velantine Le Long documented her bike ride from Chicago to San Francisco for the *San Francisco Chronicle*.

Chris Carlsson travels the globe helping other countries organize Critical Mass rides.

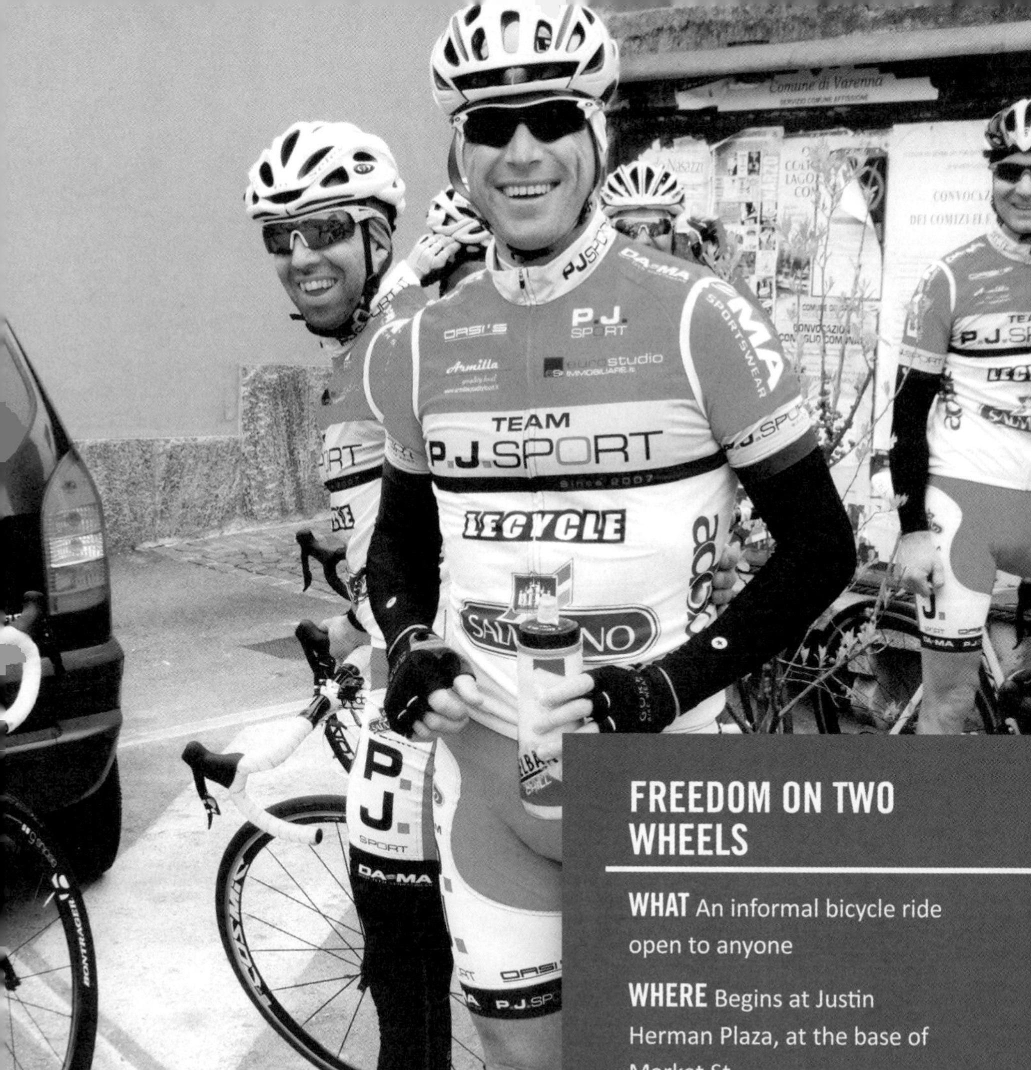

Critical Mass has spread around the globe.

FREEDOM ON TWO WHEELS

WHAT An informal bicycle ride open to anyone

WHERE Begins at Justin Herman Plaza, at the base of Market St.

COST Free, just show up with your bike.

PRO TIP If you plan on driving on the last Friday evening of the month avoid the downtown or expect delays.

Critical Mass has received some bad press in the past. In 1997, five thousand bikers lined the streets during commuting hours, leading to screaming matches with drivers, blocked intersections, and many arrests. It has since evolved into smaller, calmer bike rides.

60 HISTORIC HIJINKS

Are the plaques displayed around San Francisco accurate?

Before the Comedy Channel TV show *Drunk History* there were Clampers. Members of E Clampus Vitus—Clampers for short—say they are either historians that like to drink or drunks that like history. Their motto is: "I believe because it is absurd."

It's an all-male group spoofing traditional fraternal organizations such as the Masons, claims Robert Chandler, an ex-noble Grand Humbug (which means he served as president). He's written a book, *An E Clampus Vitus Hoax Goes Awry*, about a joke that got out of hand.

In the 1930s Clampers member Henry Bolton, a U.C. Berkeley history professor, was obsessed with the legendary story that Sir Francis Drake discovered San Francisco and left behind a plaque. The Clampers went to great lengths to create a realistic brass plaque and then dumped it in the Bay. It was discovered and found its way to Professor Bolton who was convinced it was the real thing. Many experts agreed

DRUNK HISTORY

WHAT Plaques put up by Clampers

WHERE Many bars in town including The Saloon and the Old Ship Saloon.

COST Free

PRO TIP After viewing the plaque at Anchor Brewing Company on Potrero Hill, check out their store. It sells beer you can't find anywhere else.

The Sir Francis Drake hotel doormen wear Beefeater uniforms, but the establishment does not sport the infamous plaque.

THE
SALOON
Here before you is the oldest saloon in San Francisco. Alsatian immigrant Ferdinand E. Wagner ran a fruit store in this building from 1858 to 1859, later transforming it into "Wagner's Beer Hall" in 1860. Taking over for his father in 1869, Edward Wagner successfully ran the establishment until its sale in 1884.
This saloon has had numerous owners over the years, surviving the 1906 earthquake with the help of San Francisco firemen and/or Navy crews. It then survived Prohibition by being renamed from "The Poodle Dog Saloon" to the prohibition name "The Poodle Dog Cafe".
With the repeal in 1933, this establishment was once again a beer garden, changing names a few more times until it became just simply and rightly so "The Saloon" in 1984.
CREDO QUIA ABSURDUM
Dedicated on March 28, 2014
Yerba Buena Lodge No. 1,
E Clampsus Vitus
Satisfactory

During the Gold Rush the Clampers were known for helping "widders" and orphans.

and the truth didn't emerge for decades even though they Clampers had inscribed a small EVC insignia on the back.

Today Clampers plaques are on display around the city. Members get permission from the owners before hanging the signs but sometimes the proprietors embellish their heritage. "We've put up more plaques in CA than any other organization, "says Chandler. As to whether the signs are accurate, he says, "We do the best research we can and try for accuracy, but it depends on the humor of the Humbug, and intentionally or otherwise, sometimes things are wrong."

61 TAP IT

Why did San Francisco bottle its water?

When you're in a San Francisco restaurant and the waiter asks what water you'd prefer request the Hetch Hetchy. It won't be on the menu but they'll have it.

Never heard of it? Don't feel bad; it's San Francisco's tap water, from the pristine snowmelts and waterfalls of Yosemite National Park, delivered via the Hetch Hetchy reservoir. In national competitions San Francisco repeatedly wins first place for the best tasting tap water, which led former Mayor Willie Brown to bottle more than thirty thousand bottles in 2003 as a publicity stunt. While the bottled water experiment was short-lived, it spurred a law prohibiting San Francisco government agencies from purchasing bottled water.

Recently a river restoration plan that would require giving up some of the city's Hetch Hetchy water was strongly opposed by Mayor London Breed.

If you're curious about how the Hetch Hetchy water travels two hundred miles from Yosemite to San Francisco, check out the digital art walls at the new headquarters of the San Francisco Public Utilities Commission.

Willie Brown was a flamboyant mayor who also served in the CA state legislature and currently writes a column for the *San Francisco Chronicle*.

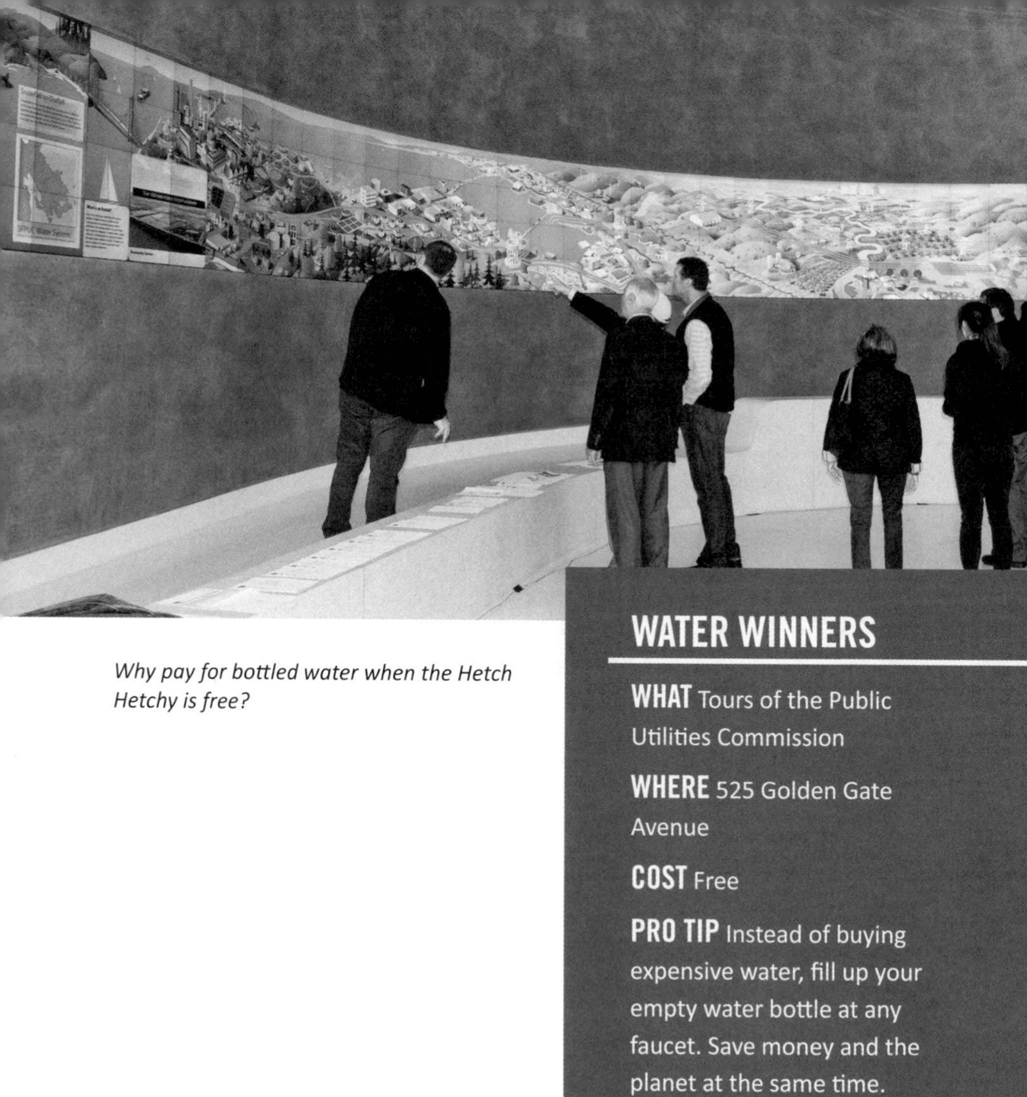

Why pay for bottled water when the Hetch Hetchy is free?

WATER WINNERS

WHAT Tours of the Public Utilities Commission

WHERE 525 Golden Gate Avenue

COST Free

PRO TIP Instead of buying expensive water, fill up your empty water bottle at any faucet. Save money and the planet at the same time.

62 LEAVING A LEGACY

Where can I find the "real" San Francisco?

When the Gold Dust Lounge and Lefty O'Doul's closed the earth shook but it wasn't an earthquake—it was locals demanding the city do something to protect what makes it unique. Besides rock and roll, this city was built on Barbary Coast bohemian charm but the city was becoming a victim of its own success. Iconic spots were shutting down due to new developments and skyrocketing rents.

Inspired by a Buenos Aires program that awards cultural significance status to cafes, bars, and businesses, the San Francisco Heritage Society partnered with the city to create the first Legacy Business Registry in the country. Approved by voters in 2015, it gives special status to any business that has operated in San Francisco for thirty years, but it goes beyond saving brick and mortar to include contributions to a neighborhood's history or identity. Mike Buhler, president of San Francisco Heritage, said, "We realized you can save a landmark building, but that won't keep the intangible things that make the city special like the quirky regulars."

SAN FRANCISCO'S SOUL

WHAT Legacy Businesses

WHERE All over the city

COST Varies depending on venue

PRO TIP For a list of all the legacy businesses, visit sanfranciscoheritage.org.

Before the Legacy Business legislation actor Sean Penn stepped in to save Tosca Café when it was in danger of closing.

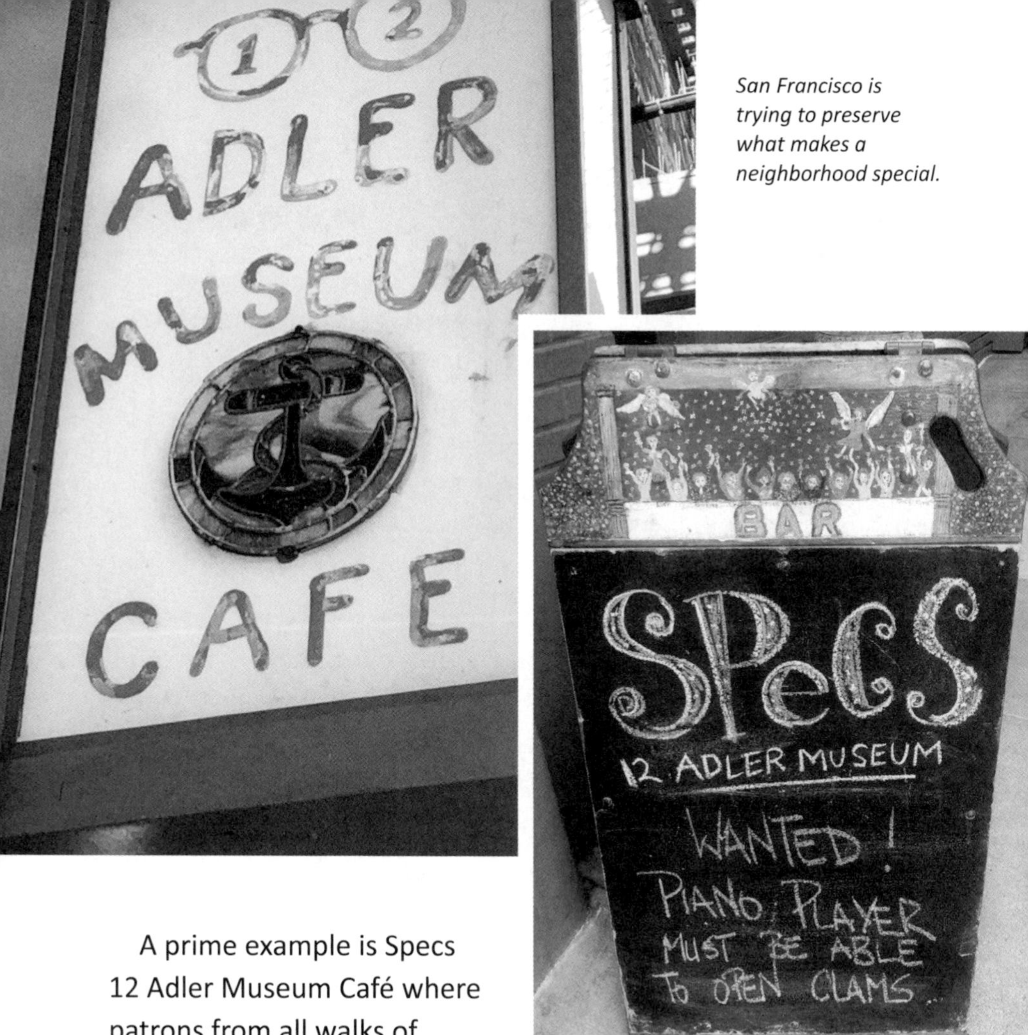

San Francisco is trying to preserve what makes a neighborhood special.

A prime example is Specs 12 Adler Museum Café where patrons from all walks of life brought the late Richard "Specs" Simmons unusual gifts from their trips. The objects on display in his bar include a whale eardrum, Spanish Civil War posters, antique maps of Chinatown, a framed article about Simmons' brush with death when his ship sank, and a mummy. One of Specs favorite phrases was, "If you want better service keep moving."

63 BANK ON IT

Where is the most gorgeous place to deposit your money?

Be prepared . . . walking into this Italian renaissance building will cause your jaw to drop and your hand to reach for your iPhone camera. You'll be mesmerized by the rays filtering through the rotunda onto the opulent lobby where a curved white staircase, granite pillars, marble counters, and teller windows made of bronze compete for your attention. This is the most beautiful Wells Fargo bank in the country.

Anyone would feel safe depositing money here and that was the idea. To open the vault downstairs employees have to swing a huge wheel that looks like a movie prop and it was used in several films, most recently a documentary on Batkid.

When the original owner, Charles Crocker hired architect William Polk in 1908, he told him to spare no expense. Crocker was a member of the Big Four, the tycoons that built the Central Pacific Railway and lived on Nob Hill, a shortened form of the Hindu word nabob which describes a European who made a large fortune. In 1882 Robert Louis Stevenson described it as the hill of palaces. Crocker wanted the entire block for his estate and when a family refused to sell Crocker built a "spite fence" cutting off the view and light from his

---

Another member of the Big Four, Leland Stanford, co-founded the University bearing his name after his son died and Harvard, mistaking him for a hick, turned him away.

This bank lured customers with marble and gold.

MAKE A DEPOSIT

WHAT Original Crocker Bank

WHERE One Montgomery

COST Free

PRO TIP Visit the Wells Fargo Museum at 420 Montgomery St. where you can learn how to drive a stagecoach, use vintage bank machines, and send a telegram to another museum.

neighbor. It was difficult for the horses and residents to climb up steep Snob Hill (its current nickname), so in 1878 these "Robber Barons" installed their own cable car line that you can still ride today.

In the 1980s Wells Fargo absorbed Crocker Bank, but thankfully they preserved the original architecture.

64 SHELL GAME

Where can you see San Francisco history in one block?

Booms and busts have always been a part of San Francisco, and there's proof of that on one block in the Financial District. Bush Street has three architectural marvels reflecting the times: a building constructed after the 1906 quake, an ornate corporate palace from the Roaring '20s, and a mid-century modernist marvel.

The story starts with "The Suspender Building." Constructed in 1910 after the big quake, this factory at 130 Bush Street was purposefully thin to advertise the products: belts and ties and suspenders. Down the block, Shell Oil also promoted their product on the outside of a terra cotta high-rise. Money was no object in 1929 and it shows on Shell's ornate building at 100 Bush Street. Look closely and you'll notice oil geysers carved into the sandstone walls leading to the roof, topped by (what else) shells.

Most construction stopped during the Great Depression but it came back with a vengeance in the 1950s.

Acclaimed architect Mies Van Der Rohe, known for the saying "less is more," took note of the Hallidie Building and built a wall of glass at One Bush Plaza. The former headquarters for the Crown Zellerbach paper company, it was one of the first buildings set back from the street. The glass cube-shaped lobby appears to be holding up the building.

The Shell Building has one of the best POPOS (privately owned public open spaces). Located at street level, it's a palm tree oasis with a café and plenty of tables and chairs.

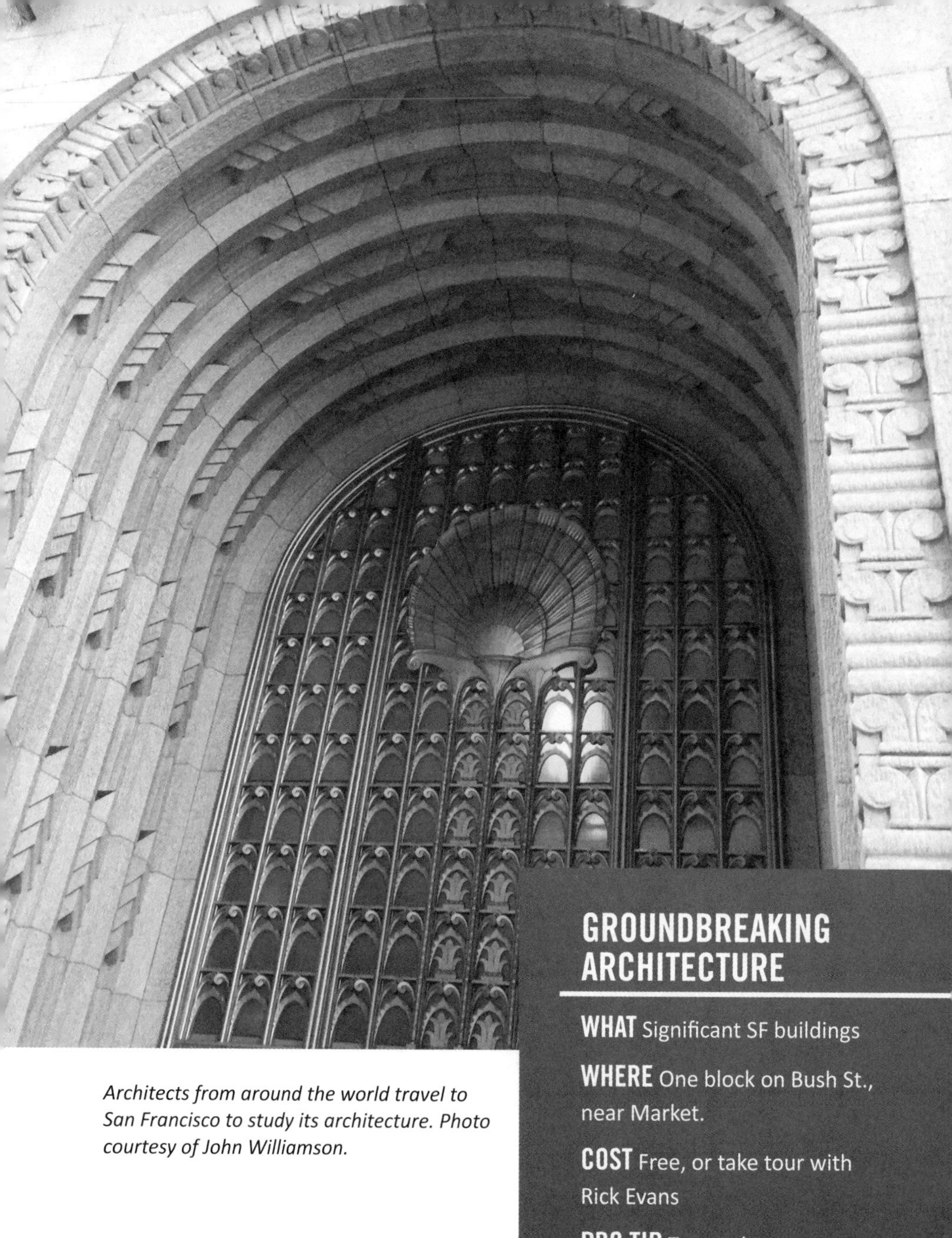

Architects from around the world travel to San Francisco to study its architecture. Photo courtesy of John Williamson.

GROUNDBREAKING ARCHITECTURE

WHAT Significant SF buildings

WHERE One block on Bush St., near Market.

COST Free, or take tour with Rick Evans

PRO TIP To see the juxtaposition of old and new, take a photo of the Shell structure reflected in the glass windows of the Crown Zellerbach Building.

65 IMPOSTER

Is Lombard Street's claim to fame a lie?

Tourists from around the world gather there every day: gawking, taking photos, walking, biking, and driving down Lombard, which they believe is the crookedest street in the world. But it's not even the crookedest street in San Francisco!

That title goes to Vermont Street on Potrero Hill, according to the Public Works Department. Vermont Street is steeper—a 14.3 percent grade with a tighter turning radius and fewer turns than Lombard. Vermont Street isn't as pretty (it's on concrete not cobblestones) and it's not lined with flowers, but it does have an annual tricycle race.

Every Easter Sunday the Bring Your Own Big Wheel race takes place on Vermont Street. Kids of all ages ride down the crooked street on plastic tricycles. It started in 2000 when Jon Brumit came across an abandoned big wheel and decided he'd cruise down Lombard. He passed out fliers encouraging neighbors to join him but the day of the race he was the only one who showed up. Afterward, however, word spread, and each year more people joined him in zigzagging down the brick street until the event became too big for the neighborhood. In 2008 the Big Wheel Race moved to Vermont Street.

GRADE A

WHAT Bring Your Own Big Wheel race

WHERE Vermont St. between 20th and 22nd Sts.

COST Free

PRO TIP The first hour of the event is kids-only racing.

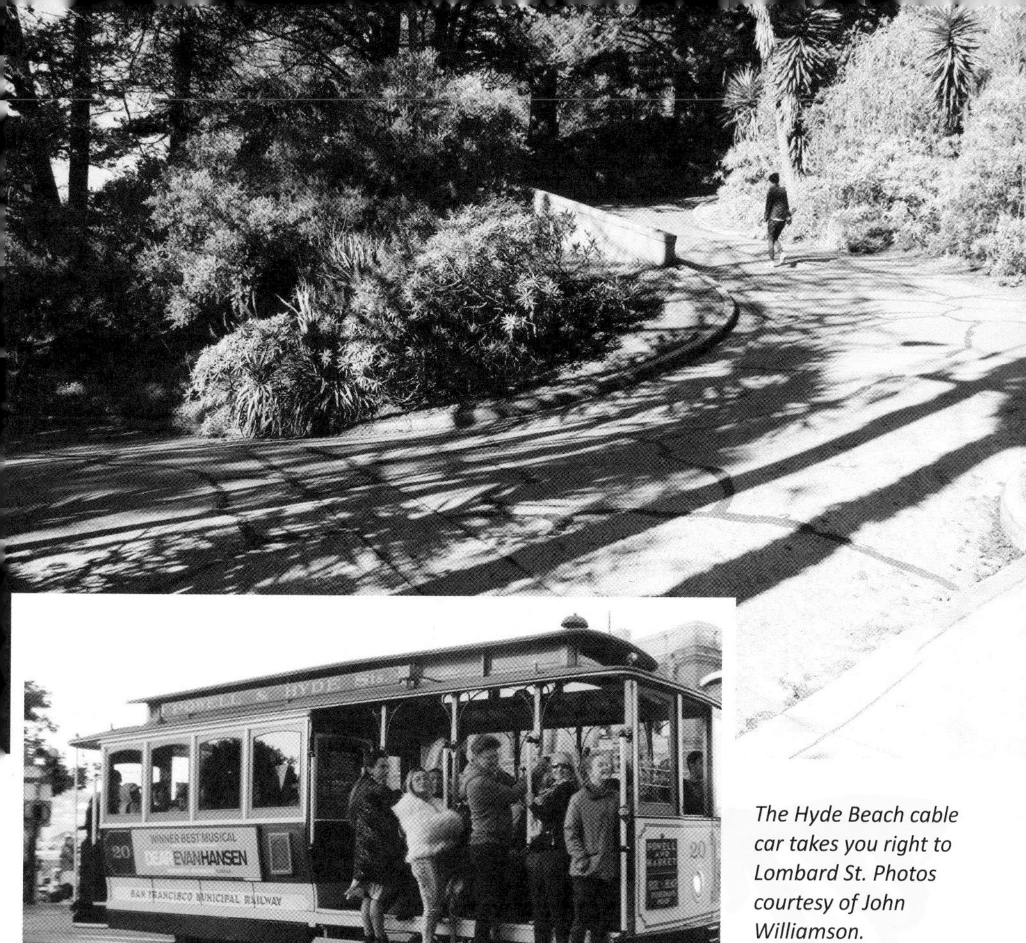

The Hyde Beach cable car takes you right to Lombard St. Photos courtesy of John Williamson.

Too many tourists are causing headaches for Lombard residents, and the city is considering charging cars to drive down the snaky road.

66 SHAKING UP SAN FRANCISCO

What forgotten building was saved by a disaster?

Before the Golden Gate and Bay Bridges were built the only way to reach the city from the East Bay and Marin was on water. The Ferry Building, which survived the 1906 quake, was essential for commuters and it was common to say, "Let's meet under the Ferry Clock."

With the combination of new bridges and fancy cars in the 1930s, the building became an abandoned relic of a bygone era. It was deemed so useless that the city built the Embarcadero Freeway in 1959, an ugly two-story structure that hid the Ferry Building. Mayor Feinstein attempted to get rid of the freeway in 1986 but voters rejected the idea. Three years later they had no choice, the 1989 earthquake severely damaged the structure and San Franciscans once again realized the treasure they had along the water.

Today it's a foodie temple filled with award-winning restaurants and local artisan shops. Each Saturday an acclaimed farmer's market takes place under the arcades and the plaza along the water. Many sellers got their start here, graduating from outdoor stands to brick and mortar stores. Be sure to walk up the grand stairway to the second floor to see the original architecture of this historic landmark, including a mosaic of the Great Seal of California.

Columnist Herb Caen wrote that the Ferry Building was his grandfather clock. The clock is the biggest wind-up, mechanical clock in the world with the largest face.

As more residents choose to commute via the water, the Ferry Building is adding more destinations. Photo courtesy of John Williamson.

RECLAIMING THE WATERFRONT

WHAT Ferry Building

WHERE 1 The Embarcadero

COST Free to walk around; restaurants and shops at all price levels.

PRO TIP Water taxis are a great way to travel along the waterfront. Look for the yellow and black checked signs.

As for those forgotten ferries? They're now the preferred choice of transportation for many commuters who prefer to relax in the bar and socialize rather than sit in traffic. Deckhands know many married couples who met while commuting on the ferry.

Tourists also enjoy boat rides; each weekend the ferry from Sausalito to San Francisco is packed with bikers who trekked across the Golden Gate Bridge and want the easy way back. The ferries service Alameda, Oakland, Larkspur, Richmond, Sausalito, and Vallejo, with plans to expand.

67 RIVERA EFFECT

Where are there priceless frescos in San Francisco?

How three Diego Rivera murals ended up in town is almost as complicated and interesting as the life story of this artist from Mexico.

Although everyone agreed that Rivera was a great artist, there were rumors that he was a communist. Despite that scandalous reputation, in 1930 some leading San Franciscans—William Gerstle, president of the San Francisco Art Institute, and Timothy Pflueger, architect for the Pacific Coast Stock Exchange—took the risk of inviting him here.

Rivera's mural for the Stock Exchange (now the City Club), angered local artists who thought it hypocritical to commission a communist for a building honoring capitalism. His thirty-foot-high fresco, *Allegory of California*, also called *Riches of California*, was the first mural Rivera painted in the U.S.

The San Francisco Art Institute mural was controversial because Rivera painted himself sitting on a scaffold with his butt facing the audience and some felt that was an insult, although Rivera denied that was his intention.

Despite these concerns, people were impressed enough with the murals to invite Rivera back to the city for the Golden Gate International Exposition on

MURALS FOR THE MASSES

WHAT Diego Rivera frescos

WHERE City Club, Academy of Art institute, CCSF and—in 2020—SFMOMA.

COST Free

PRO TIP City Guides offers free tours of the Rivera fresco at the private City Club.

Rivera is often credited with inspiring the murals decorating buildings in the Mission District.

Visitors to the World's Fair on Treasure Island were able to see Rivera at work.

Treasure Island where he created *Pan American Unity*. In this fresco his back is also turned—to his ex-wife Frieda Kahlo—while he faces his lover, movie star Paulette Goddard, who was married to Charlie Chaplin. Kahlo also exhibited her art at the World's Fair and the two artists decided to remarry here, with one caveat: Kahlo insisted the union would be sexless.

After the expo the mural was relocated to Community College of San Francisco (CCSF). In 2020 this mural will be temporarily moved to SF Museum of Modern Art as the centerpiece of a major exhibition of Rivera's work. It will be located on the street level in a space free and open to the public, as Diego would have wanted it.

68 MAINLAND HAWAII

Where in California do they say "aloha" instead of "hello"?

There's a place in the Bay Area where restaurants serve seaweed, the university teaches hula dancing, and there are free ukulele concerts on the beach.

Located about an hour and a half south of San Francisco, Santa Cruz has a history with the Hawaiian Islands dating back to 1883. King Kalakaua's three nephews—David, Jonah, and Edward—had surfboards made from redwood trees and tried them out in Santa Cruz.

Although locals quickly adopted surfing, it wasn't until recently that the city embraced all things Hawaiian. There are authentic Hawaiian restaurants, a Hawaiian boutique, and a Hawaiian home store. But the biggest thing you'll notice is the sound . . . everyone seems to be playing the ukulele, an instrument resembling a mini-guitar. Some grade schools are even giving students ukulele lessons as part of a lesson on Hawaiian culture.

There are free concerts all over the area:

Capitola bandstand on Sunday, Yacht Harbor beach Saturday and Wednesday mornings, Pono Hawaiian Grill the first Tuesdays of the month, and Food Lounge on the first Thursday of the month.

Woodies on the Wharf is an annual event drawing big crowds to see these iconic cars and mingle with the surfing culture.

Ukuleles are an inexpensive instrument and easy to learn! Photo courtesy of Julie E. Hendricks.

The biggest musical gathering takes place the third Thursday of every month when the Ukulele Club plays at Bocci Cellar. These meetings are free and open to everyone. Ukes are available for beginners and there's often a guest performer from Hawaii.

A HAWAIIAN EXPERIENCE

WHAT Ukulele concerts

WHERE Bocci Cellars, Yacht Harbor Beach, Capitola bandstand, Pono Hawaiian Grill, and the Food Lounge

COST Free

PRO TIP If you're driving down Highway One from SF grab a bite at the famous Taco Bell on the beach in Pacifica. It's called the most beautiful chain restaurant in the United States. Thanks to social media attention it was recently remodeled—surfers love the walk-up window—and will serve alcohol!

69 THE FRENCH CONNECTION

Why is San Francisco the Paris of the Pacific?

Ooh la la! The French used fashion and flair to make a lasting impact on a fledgling San Francisco. Before Chinatown there was a Frenchtown, strategically located on the wharf. When ships landed, passengers found French restaurants, card houses, and the latest Parisian fashions.

These commodities were in high demand. Travelers lured by the gold rush found a small town with few goods and were so desperate for supplies they stormed incoming cargo ships. "When Frenchman Emile Verdier arrived, he was shocked to find all his merchandise sold before he even stepped off the boat," says Gilles Lorand, the only French-speaking tour guide in San Francisco, www.sanfranciscobygilles.com.

Recognizing the opportunity, Verdier opened The City of Paris, one of San Francisco's most important department stores. His fellow countryman Raphael Weill founded the White House department store.

After the 1906 earthquake Weill became a local hero. He sent his Parisian cousin a telegram requesting an immediate delivery of clothing, offering to pay whatever it cost. When the shipment arrived, Weill gave all the garments away to women and children.

The French Hospital was the country's first HMO (health maintenance organization). For a dollar a month patients received health care and free drinks! French Hospital eventually became Kaiser, the largest HMO in the world.

San Francisco remembers their French friends—there are many Bastille day events. Photo courtesy of John Williamson.

SAVOIR FAIRE

WHAT The City of Paris rotunda

WHERE Neiman Marcus, 150 Stockton St.

COST Free to look, but be forewarned: the store's nickname is Needless Markup.

PRO TIP Belden Alley, filled with French restaurants, is nicknamed the French Quarter.

The Beaux-Arts buildings are still on Union Square, but the names have changed. The White House is a Banana Republic, and Neiman Marcus is located on the former City of Paris site. Neiman's kept the City of Paris tradition, a towering Christmas tree in the lobby. Most importantly, they preserved the stained-glass rotunda. Look closely and you'll see the motto below the ship, "fluctuate nec mergitur." Translation: "It floats and never sinks," the coat of arms for Paris.

This was also an appropriate slogan for the French immigrants seeking gold in their adopted city. Those who didn't strike it rich in the mines stayed afloat when they realized the real treasure was the city itself.

70 WHEN BLUE COLLARS BEAT BLUE BLOODS

How did San Francisco come to host the America's Cup?

When Larry Ellison, the Oracle CEO, decided to enter the America's Cup sailing race he approached the elite St. Francis Yacht Club to sponsor the team. It seemed a given that the St. Francis would embrace this opportunity; money was no object with Ellison's deep pockets, and it would be a first for San Francisco to win what many consider the most prestigious international sailing race. Surprisingly, the Club turned Ellison down, reportedly due to control issues.

Just down the road the Golden Gate Yacht Club (GGYC) was so deeply in debt it was considering closing. When Commodore Norbert Bajurin learned St. Francis rejected Ellison, he quickly offered GGYC. Ellison not only took him up on the offer, he also paid off the club's debts, enrolled his team as members, and remodeled the Club.

ANCHORS AWEIGH

WHAT Sailing on an America's Cup yacht

WHERE Pier 39, 2 Beach St.

COST Varies, check the website: acsailingsf.com

PRO TIP Show up Friday night at the GGYC dock with a six-pack of beer, and sailors claim you can join a crew in the "Beer Can" races.

Sailing races are frequent on the Bay and anyone can watch for free by bringing a blanket to Crissy Field or walking along the waterfront by the St. Francis and Golden Gate Yacht Clubs.

The Rolex Big Boat Series is another great race to watch in San Francisco.

In 2010, history was made when the coveted trophy went to the Golden Gate Yacht Club. One of the perks of winning the America's Cup is choosing the location of the next race and Oracle brought it home. Thousands of Bay Area residents lined the waterfront from Fort Mason to the Embarcadero to cheer as Oracle won again in 2013.

You can't visit GGYC unless you belong to another reciprocal yacht club, but you can sail on an America's Cup boat. Brad Webb, a bowman on the Oracle team, skippers the USA 76, an eighty-five-foot boat used in previous America's cup races. During the cruise, he encourages passengers to take the wheel and hoist the sails.

71 CHEESY EDUCATION

Where can you get schooled on cheese?

Tasting is learning, that's the philosophy behind the Cheese School of San Francisco. "We're the only independent cheese school in the nation," says owner Kiri Fisher. She's adding to the city's rich fromage history dating back to the eighteenth century.

When Father Junipero Serra was establishing missions in California, including Mission Dolores in San Francisco, he introduced the state to dairy cows and cheese making. That skill came in handy in 1865 when a poultry disease left San Francisco dockworkers without eggs for breakfast. The Marin French Cheese Company came to the rescue, creating a mild cheese the size of an egg they called Breakfast Cheese. They still sell it, but now it's called Petit Breakfast cheese.

Today the Cheese School teaches people how to make cheese, understand cheese, and—most important—enjoy cheese. Even people who hate going to school will love classes on: cheese and beer pairings, champagne and cheese, cheese and chocolate, and making a cheese pizza from scratch. In addition to classes

A TUROPHILE'S DELIGHT

WHAT Cheese School

WHERE Ghirardelli Square

COST Two-hour classes start at $69.00

PRO TIP Grab some cheese and a bottle of wine from the store and enjoy a picnic on the greens below Ghirardelli Square.

The school makes custom cheese wheel cakes popular for weddings.

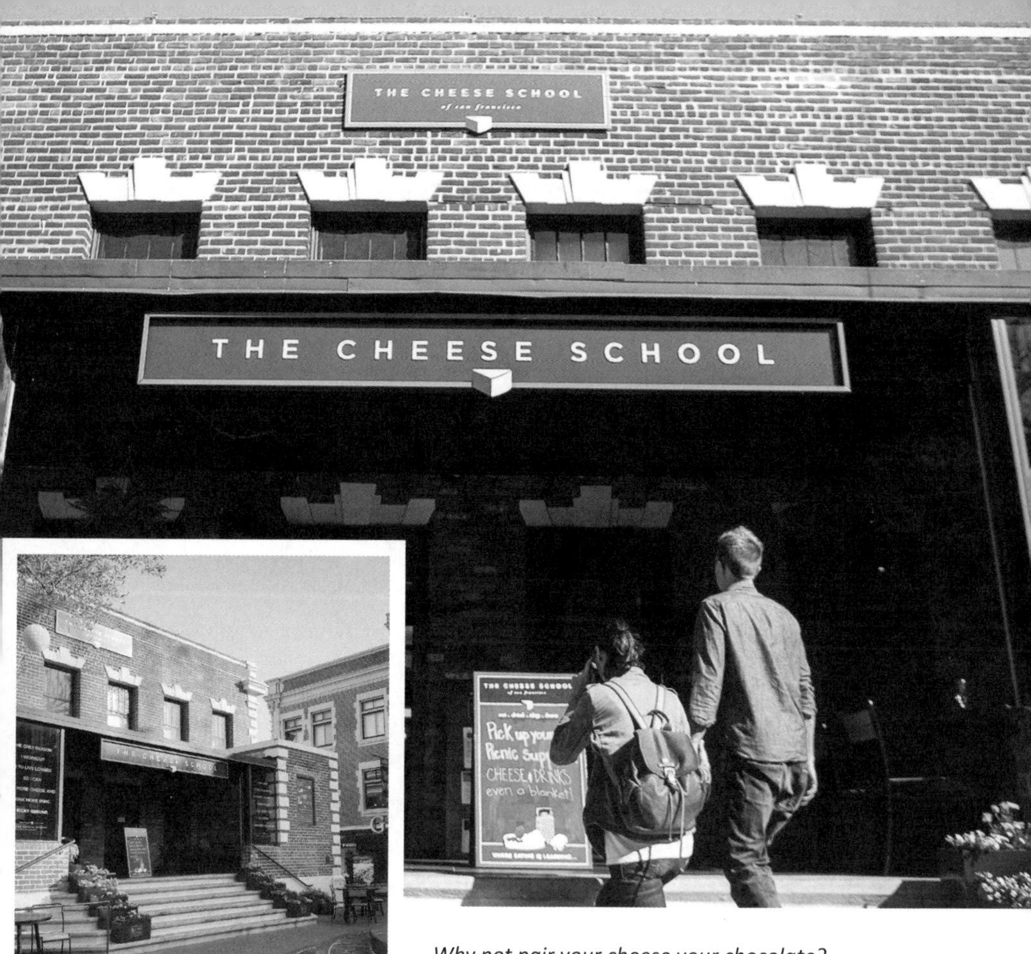

Why not pair your cheese your chocolate? Ghirardelli is right next door.

for novices there are master classes for cheesemakers and cheesemongers.

Laura Werlin, James Beard award-winning author and Cheese School instructor, says "To me the Cheese School is more like a cheese jewel. It has revolutionized the way people think about, talk about, and ultimately consumer cheese, and it's all done in a space overlooking San Francisco Bay. I call it "cheese with a view" and hands down it is my favorite place in the country to teach."

Students are able to use their newfound knowledge at the school's cheese shop and café. (Try the grilled cheese and tomato soup special).

72 SAN FRANCISCO SEND-OFF

Why is a brass band marching through Chinatown on weekends?

Most weekends in San Francisco you can watch a free concert, and free is not something to sneeze at in this uber-expensive city. Just walk through Chinatown and you'll catch The Green Street Brass Band marching through the streets—not for a parade but a funeral procession.

San Francisco has the only Chinese funeral brass marching funeral band in the world, according to Bob Yount, manager of Green Street Mortuary, and a musician himself. After he conducts the band's first song, frequently Chopin, he follows the band driving the "picture car," displaying a poster size photo of the loved one.

Although the mortuary is located in North Beach, traditionally the Italian section, residents of nearby Chinatown are the primary clients and this is the largest Chinatown in the United States.

Traditional Chinese funerals are more expensive and elaborate than even weddings possibly because legend has it that the deceased can reward families with good fortune. It's not unusual to have forty cars following the band according to Yount, who was a consultant on the TV show *Six Feet Under*.

No one knows when this unique blend of Western and Eastern funeral customs merged but it goes back as far as 1903. On YouTube you can see a video of a brass band leading a Chinese funeral in San Francisco filmed by Thomas Edison!

CHINATOWN PARADE

WHAT Green Street Marching Brass Band

WHERE Begins at Green Street Mortuary, 649 Green St. and ends at the intersection of Jackson and Kearny Sts. Most weekends four funeral processions occur from 10 a.m. to 1:30 p.m.

COST Free

PRO TIP The best viewing post is at the beginning and end of the procession.

Many famous San Franciscans request the Green St. Mortuary Marching Band Funeral.

Lisa Pollard, aka the Sax Lady, leads the ten-piece member band whose members have played with musicians like Huey Lewis and Stan Kenton. "We try to be perfect; we owe them that," she says.

A San Francisco send-off should be extra special if you believe Herb Caen, the former columnist for the San Francisco Chronicle. One of his famous quotes is, "One day if I do go to heaven, I'll look around and say, it ain't bad, but it ain't San Francisco."

73 URBAN JUNGLE

Why are wild animals roaming the city?

There's a culture clash in San Francisco and this time it's not between hippies and the establishment—it's between people and wild animals. There appears to be an increase in the number of mountain lions, coyotes, and foxes sharing space with two-legged creatures, according to Deb Campbell, spokesperson for the city's animal control department. Golden Gate Bridge workers have seen coyotes walk by their toll booths and Salesforce CEO Marc Benioff shared video of a mountain lion hanging out in his Pacific Heights backyard.

The Presidio Trust placed GPS tracking devices on the coyotes living on the former military base to better understand these animals. "One night we received numerous calls from people about coyote sightings," says Campbell. "We thought there were eight coyotes roaming the streets but we found out from the tracking that it was just one who went for a long walk." Campbell estimates there are dozens of coyotes in San Francisco and they're here to stay. It's illegal to shoot them, they don't fall for traps, and even if they did more would appear, she says.

"San Francisco is a convenient place for them to live. They have water, shelter, and access to food. Every city has seen an increase and they're wily coyotes." One of their food sources is little dogs, so people should leash their pets, she warns. Coyotes are friendly so some people feed them, which is the worst thing you can do. "Pretty soon they look to people

---

Campbell says that people are afraid of coyotes but there are no reports of coyotes biting people in San Francisco and eight hundred reports a year of dogs biting people.

COYOTE ALERT
COYOTES HAVE RECENTLY BEEN SEEN IN THIS AREA
SF Parks are an urban refuge for several hundred species of wildlife. You may even encounter a coyote, a native to California and still present in natural areas in the greater Bay Area. Just like the other creatures which live here, coyotes are naturally wary of people but are wild animals and should be treated with appropriate re-spect. By following park rules, people can co-exist harmoniously with wildlife.
PARK WILDLIFE GUIDELINES
THE PARK'S RULES AND REGULATIONS FUNCTION TO PROTECT PEOPLE, PETS, AND WILDLIFE
Keep your distance from coyotes. Neither adults nor children should approach or feed wildlife of any kind.
Although coyotes are typically most active in the
mornings; they can be active throughout
your surroundings.
If you are a pet owner, keep your pet
when it is outdoors.
If you have an encounter with a
the animal by loud

Racoons and possums are also a problem in San Francisco.

SF'S WILD SIDE

WHAT Wildlife sightings in the Bay Area

WHERE Primarily areas with a lot of land such as Golden Gate Park and the Presidio but people have seen them on Telegraph Hill and walking down streets.

COST Free

PRO TIP Get a guaranteed sighting of wildlife at the San Francisco Zoo.

for food and feel comfortable approaching them," says Campbell.

As for the danger these animals pose, mountain lions in neighborhoods are shot with tranquilizer guns and relocated to open spaces, according to Campbell. Warning signs are posted in areas where coyotes have been sighted, but Campbell says they usually don't threaten humans. If a coyote does follow you, she recommends yelling and raising your arms to appear large just like you would with bears, which haven't been spotted in the city . . . yet.

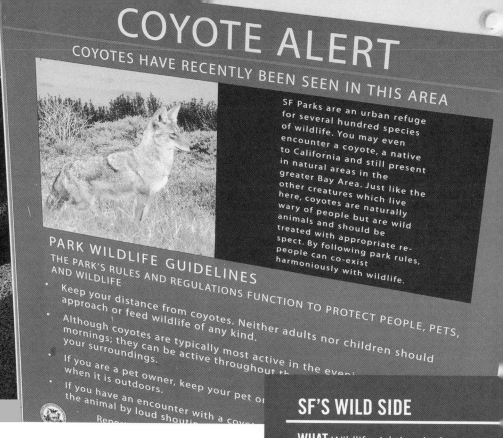

74 SOUNDS OF SAN FRANCISCO

Can you see sound?

Sitting in a circle, in total darkness, enveloped in sound, feels like being in a cocoon. Your entire being is immersed in absorbing the sounds: footsteps, trains, and raindrops, transmitted through 176 speakers in the walls, ceilings, and floor.

A new tech invention? Nah. Audium, a theater of sculptured sound, has been around since the 1950s, before anyone even thought of surround sound at the movies. It's the only theater created specifically for capturing sound movement.

It was created by Stan Shaff, a classically trained musician, and Doug McEachern who designed the equipment. Today Shaff and his son Dave, also a musician, operate the theater and compose symphonies of everyday noises like wind gusts, horns, and whispers. In today's digital age a popular attraction without images is shocking and rewarding: you create a movie in your mind to match the sounds.

A half hour before the show there's a line outside the wooden building. There are no windows, a small sign, and heavy wooden oversize doors. It feels slightly illicit, like entering a speakeasy. When I asked Dave why people would line up for a show where they aren't going to see anything

---

Previously the building was a bakery with a huge donut sign hanging out front. Stan Schaff wanted to keep the donut, but it was damaged during renovations.

Sometimes sounds are more moving than pictures. Photo courtesy of Kim Huynh.

THE THEATER OF SCULPTURED SOUND

WHAT Audium, a sound theater

WHERE 1616 Bush St.

COST $20.00

PRO TIP No children under twelve are admitted, and the "concert" is only given on the weekends.

(does it really matter where you sit?), he said it's because they usually sell out.

Technology is finally catching up to the pioneering Audium, and the theater is considering creating a residency program to assist artists in learning how to work with immersive sound.

75 DUTCH TREAT

Where can you find a hint of Holland in the city?

San Francisco has a history of tilting at windmills but it's still surprising when you run across two gigantic ones in Golden Gate Park.

The San Francisco Giants, as the Netherlands refer to them, are made for Instagram, but that wasn't their original purpose. Golden Gate Park was transformed from sand dunes to green grass through irrigation, but it was exorbitantly expensive. Windmills, powered by Pacific Ocean gusts, seemed the perfect alternative.

In 1903 the "Dutch" windmill was installed along with a home for the caretaker. According to the Golden Gate Park spokesperson, the late queen of the Netherlands, Wilhelmina, donated the Dutch windmill to the city.

It was so successful that banker Samuel Murphy donated money to build a second windmill. The Murphy windmill was the largest in the world, with 114-foot sails, each cut from a single log. Interestingly, these sails turned clockwise while traditional windmills turn counterclockwise.

It got lots of attention: In 1921 daredevil Velma Tilden climbed aboard those sails and held on for twenty-five rotations to win twenty-five dollars' worth of chocolates, and it was featured in the Charlie Chaplin movie *A Jitney Elopement*.

Electric pumps soon made the windmills obsolete, but by then they were part of the landscape. Over the years the windmills deteriorated, mechanical parts were pillaged during World War II, and the Murphy sails fell to the ground.

Visit in early spring to see tulips in bloom at the Queen Wilhelmina Garden.

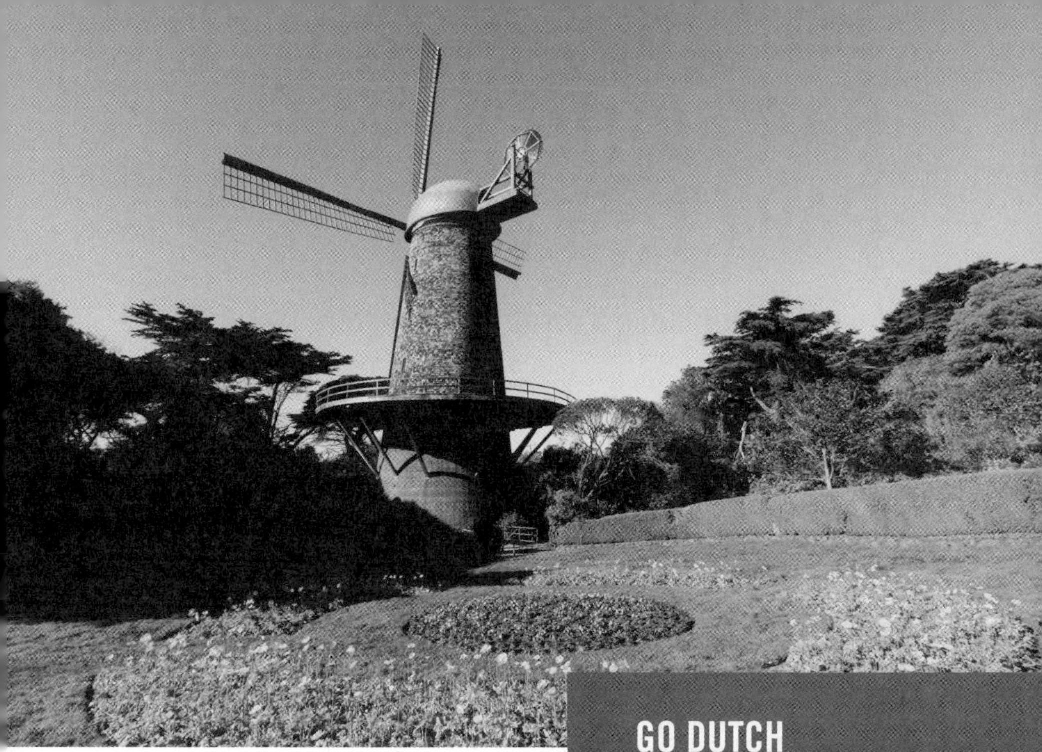

No need to go Dutch visiting the windmills—it's free. Photo courtesy of John Williamson.

Recently their inner workings were re-fitted in the Netherlands by a centuries-old windmill designer and now the Park and Rec department conducts weekly maintenance. There are plans to create a walking/biking path between the two windmills.

GO DUTCH

WHAT Authentic, gigantic windmills

WHERE Golden Gate Park

COST Free

PRO TIP After touring the windmills, cross the street to see the WPA murals at the Beach Chalet restaurant.

76 BARS WITH A STORY PART I

Where can you have a drink and a history lesson at the same time?

Barbary Coast saloons, speakeasies, and beatnik bars . . . these drinking establishments all played a role in forming San Francisco. You can feel good about raising a glass in these establishments; you're helping preserve the city's legacy! Booze has played such a role in the city's history I've had to break this entry into two parts, 1851 and after.

The Old Ship Saloon—This is not a gimmicky name; it comes from its unique origins. In 1849 a ship crashed into Alcatraz and was towed to what is now Pacific and Battery. San Franciscans being what they are, in 1851 they put up a gangplank and turned the schooner into a bar popular with sailors, miners, gamblers and bootleggers. Like all the abandoned boats during the Gold Rush, the ship was covered over by landfill, but a brick and mortar bar exists above it. During recent renovations, the owners discovered a large wooden piece of the ship they plan to display . . . it will fit right in with the nautical decor. The bartenders are happy to tell you stories of the saloon's illustrious past, including shanghaiing.

I'LL DRINK TO THAT

WHAT Bars with a story

WHERE The Old Ship Saloon, 298 Pacific Ave.; The Saloon, 1232 Grant St.

COST Moderate

PRO TIP At the Old Ship Saloon ask for a Pisco punch; it was invented here.

Boz Scaggs used to show up at The Saloon unannounced and perform.

While renovating The Old Ship Saloon recently discovered part of an old schooner.

The Saloon—It claims to be the oldest bar in San Francisco and it's one of the few buildings that survived the fire after the 1906 earthquake. Legend has it firefighters were especially motivated to save The Saloon because they frequented its upstairs brothel. This blues venue is a dive bar with a wooden floor, a two-drink minimum, and some quirky regulars. One called the Saloon his living room, while another regular dances like a pro and asks every woman to join him.

77 BARS WITH A STORY PART II

What are some of the most unusual waterholes in the city?

The place where time stands still is the nickname for the House of Shields. Since opening in 1908, this mahogany-lined saloon with brass chandeliers has never had a clock on the wall (or a TV for that matter). A speakeasy during Prohibition, legend has it there were secret passageways to the Palace Hotel across the street. President Warren G. Harding was a frequent visitor and according to local lore he died here, not at the Palace Hotel, but since he was with a "wanton woman" it was in everyone's best interests to cover it up. Respectable women were not allowed in the bar until the 1970s and even then only in the balcony!

With only nine bar stools, The Black Horse London Pub is the tiniest bar in San Francisco but what it lacks in size, it makes up for in fun. The bar is cash only and serves beer exclusively. Just like a speakeasy, bottles are stored in a bathtub behind the bar. The décor includes bras hanging on the wall because—the owner claims—"some women just decide to leave their undergarments."

I'LL TAKE A STORY WITH THAT DRINK

WHAT Unusual bars

WHERE House of Shields, 39 New Montgomery St.
Black Horse London Pub, 1514 Union St.

COST Depends on what you order

PRO TIP *High Spirits* by J. K. Dineen is a great guide to the legacy bars of San Francisco.

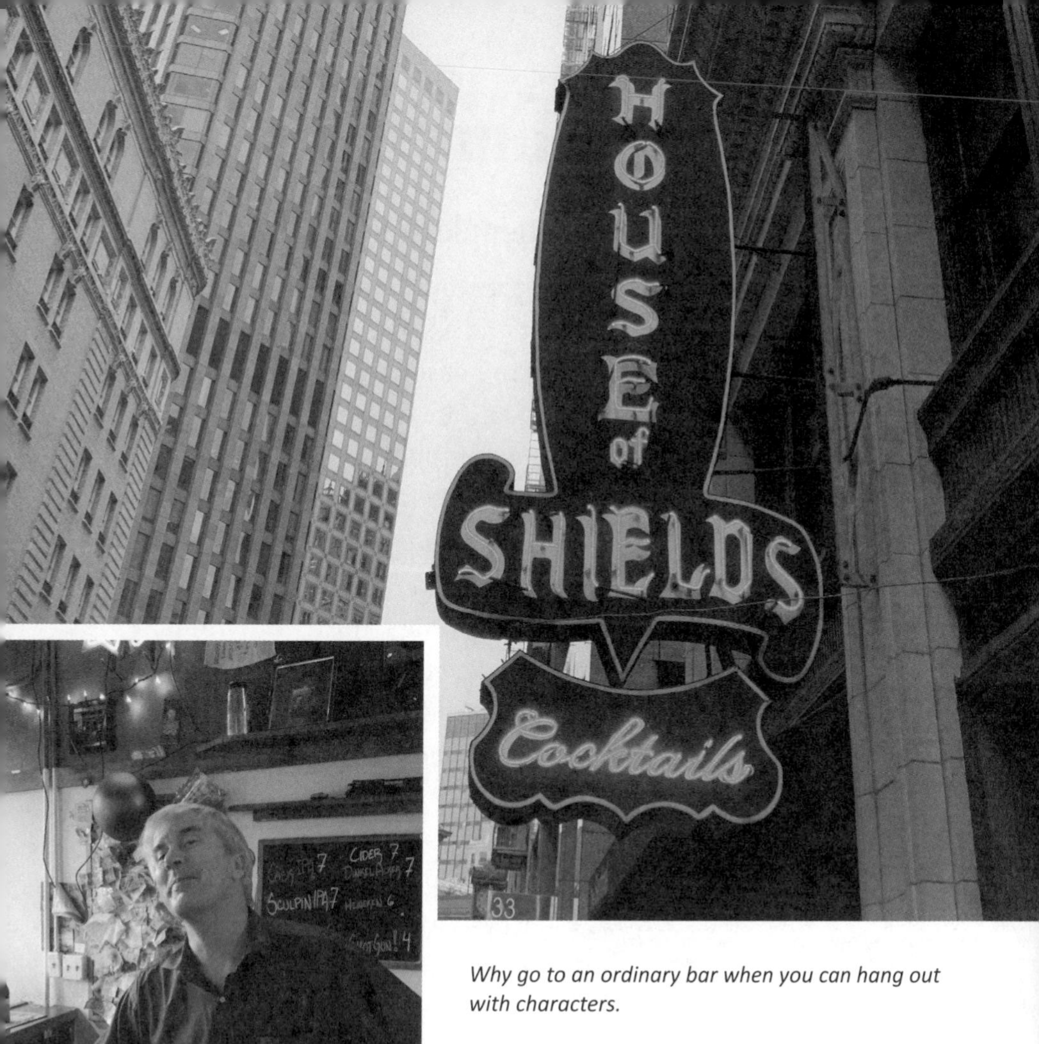

Why go to an ordinary bar when you can hang out with characters.

In the Clift Hotel the Redwood Room bar is made from a single, two-thousand-year-old Redwood tree.

78 TIN HOW TEMPLE

Where is the oldest Taoist temple in the United States?

San Francisco's Chinatown is the largest in the nation and if you leave crowded Grant Street and explore the alleyways you'll feel like you stepped into the past.

One gem is the multi-colored Tin How Temple, built in 1852. Destroyed in the 1906 quake it was rebuilt on Waverly Place. When the Chinese traveled to the Gold Mountain, their word for California during the Gold Rush, they sought protection for the long dangerous journey from Tin How, the goddess of heaven. She's known for protecting sailors, travelers, writers, and actors, according to the book *San Francisco Chinatown* by Judy Yung. Once the Chinese arrived safely in SF they built a temple to thank the goddess and ensure safe passage back home.

Visiting the Temple requires climbing up three flights of rickety stairs. You'll smell the incense before entering a narrow room decorated with lanterns adorned with red envelopes from donors, guaranteeing them a year's protection. Two women, who speak limited English, are seated at a desk, and if you ask, they'll read your fortune.

GOOD FORTUNE

WHAT Tin How Temple

WHERE 125 Waverly Place

COST Free but they have a donation box.

PRO TIP Be sure to step onto the balcony for a bird's-eye view of the Chinatown.

Each February during Chinese New Year it's traditional for Chinese families to have their fortunes read.

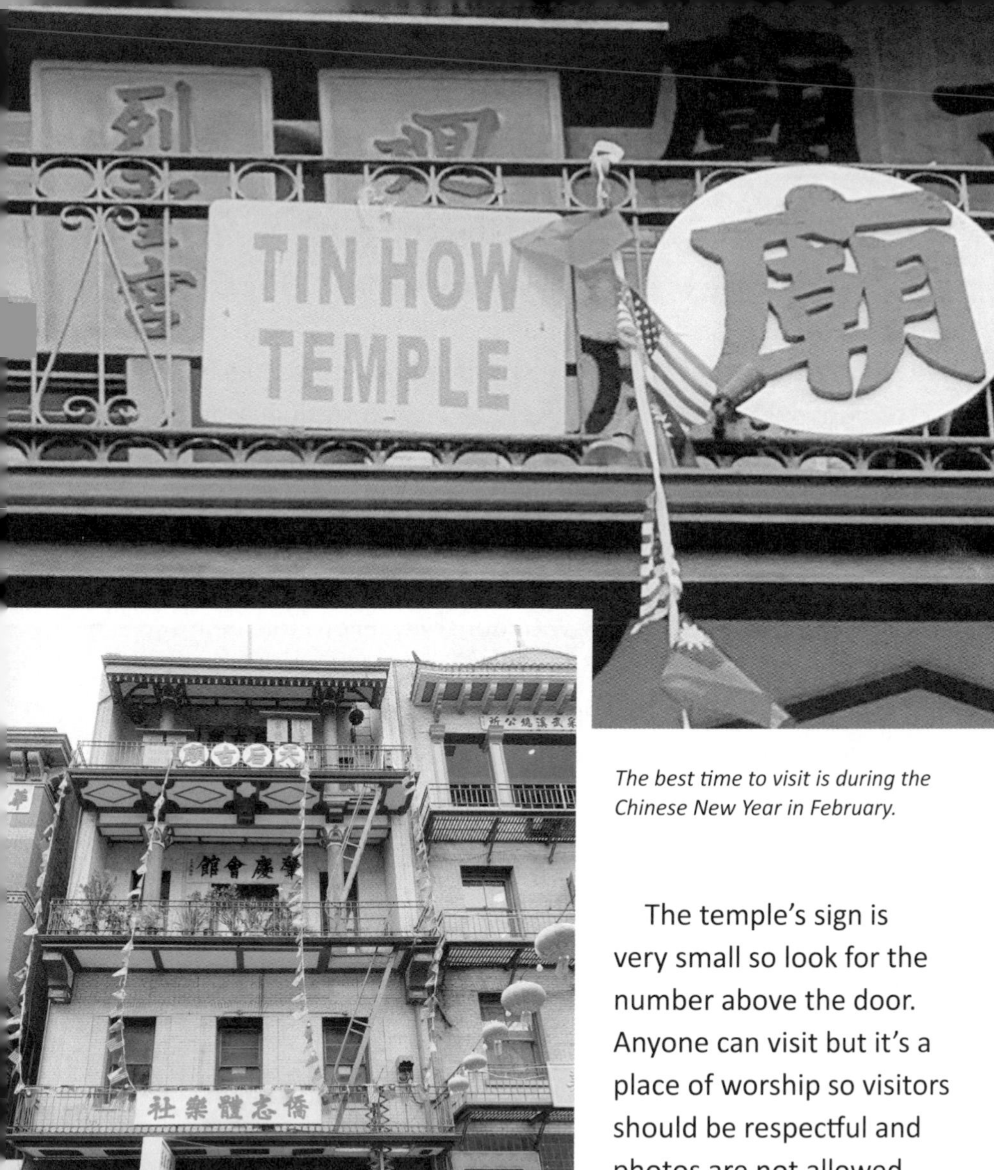

The best time to visit is during the Chinese New Year in February.

The temple's sign is very small so look for the number above the door. Anyone can visit but it's a place of worship so visitors should be respectful and photos are not allowed.

79 SEA SQUATTERS

Why did Pier 39 almost evict the sea lions?

There was a time when those adorable sea lions living on K-dock were considered a nuisance. That's right: those barking, basking beasts were considered bad neighbors. A few sea lions set up house right after the 1989 earthquake, and a year later fourteen hundred of their friends joined them, explains Sheila Chandor, Director of Marina Operations at Pier 39.

Territorial males blocked skippers from their yachts and fishermen were competing with hungry sea lions for their catch. Chandor says sea lions can eat thirty pounds of salmon a day. In addition to dealing with angry boaters, the city was worried that visitors would be scared off by the sea lions' smell and loud barking at a time when tourism was already suffering due to the devastating quake.

What no one anticipated is that the sea lions would become a huge tourist attraction. Pier 39 moved the boats and let the sea lions take over. Well not quite . . . when the sea lions "vacation" on nearby docks a Pier 39 employee gently sends them back home. "The problem is sea lions are smarter than dogs," says Chandor, "and when they see the gatekeeper walking down the docks they jump in the water. They're so clever they know when he takes his lunch, and when he leaves

---

Many people confuse sea lions with seals. The easiest ways to tell the difference: sea lions bark loudly, can walk on land using flippers, and have visible ear flaps.

You can also see sea lions at the Santa Cruz Wharf. Photo courtesy of John Williamson.

PIER 39'S BEST TOURIST ATTRACTION

WHAT Home of the sea lions

WHERE Pier 39, K Dock

COST Free

PRO TIP Pier 39 has a live sea lion webcam so you can watch them anywhere.

for the day, and that's when they jump back up on the docks."

Over the years the sea lions have made news several times: when they all disappeared overnight and just as mysteriously all returned, when the mothers gave birth on K dock instead of their usual spot at Catalina and when they bit some swimmers at nearby Aquatic ark.

It was a rocky start, but today most of the sea lions seem to enjoy being celebrities and merchants enjoy the tourists they attract.

80 CITY PAVED WITH GRAVESTONES

Why do you see dates and names on the sidewalks?

The tech boom and the resulting housing shortage are making national news, but it's not a new problem. In the 1930s land was also in short supply and mass evictions took place, but back then the residents were dead. In 1937 voters approved moving graves out of the city to nearby Colma, where they say the dead outnumber the living.

If a funeral home couldn't contact a relative, the headstones were used in construction, and tombstones, grave markers, and monuments are scattered across the city. The most visible are in Buena Vista Park, the seawalls along the Great Highway, the Marina, and Aquatic Park. You can even hear the gravestones at the Wave Organ Sculpture. Built in 1986 using tombstone remnants, the Wave Organ is activated by water hitting underground PVC pipes.

THE LIVING DEAD

WHAT Remnants of gravestones from the 1800s are embedded in the city's streets and sea walls.

WHERE Buena Vista Park: intersection of Buena Vista and Haight Sts., Great Highway Path: between Wawona St. and Lincoln along Ocean Beach, Aquatic Park, along the Marina breakwater; and at the Wave Organ, near the Golden Gate Yacht Club.

COST Free

PRO TIP Mission Dolores has one of the few cemeteries saved from the wrecking ball. You might remember it from the Hitchcock movie *Vertigo*.

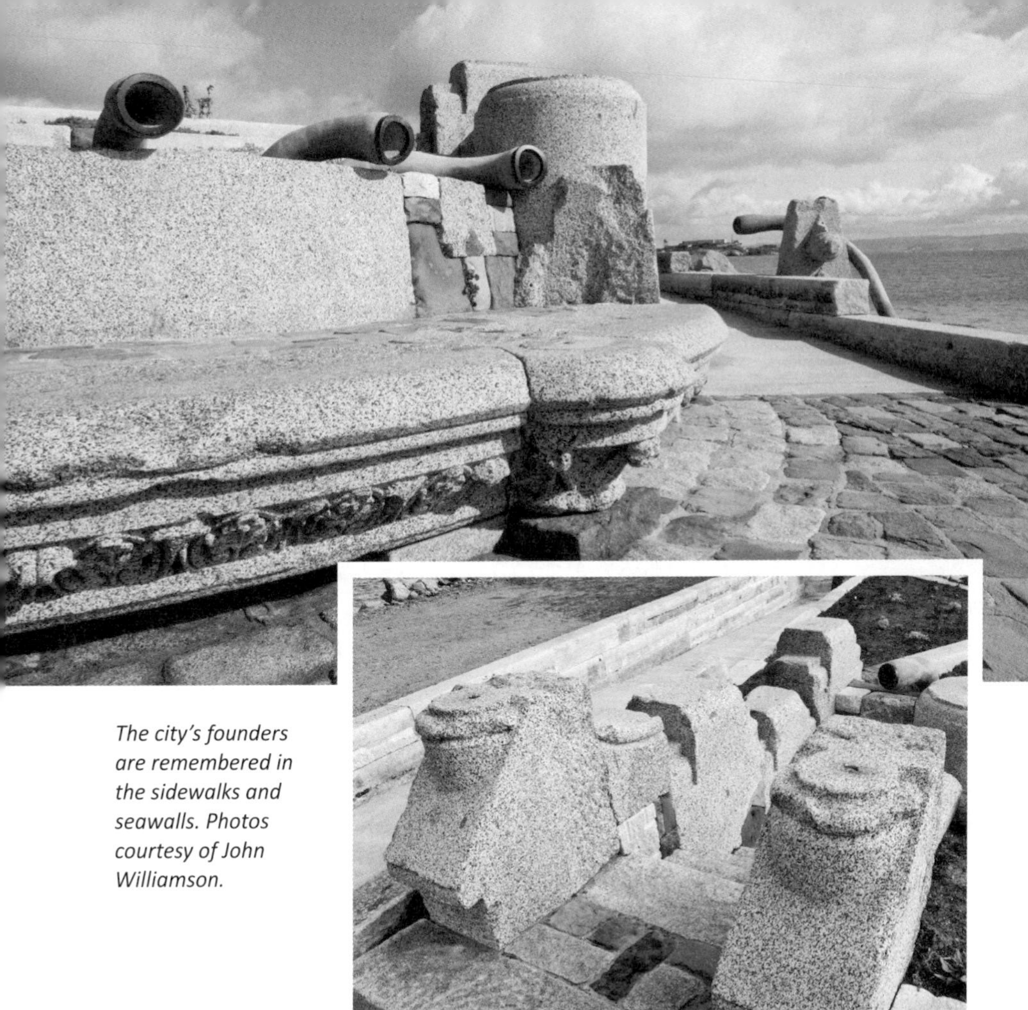

The city's founders are remembered in the sidewalks and seawalls. Photos courtesy of John Williamson.

An ornate gateway between two fairways on the Lincoln Park Golf Course is a remnant from a Chinese cemetery.

81 HOTEL OF INTERNATIONAL INTRIGUE

What secrets does this clock keep?

"Meet me under the clock," Howard Mutz tells guests at the St. Francis Hotel. It's the gathering spot for a free tour of the hotel's history encompassing movie stars, military strategies, and ladies who lunch.

Here are just a few of his stories:

One fateful Labor Day weekend in the 1920s movie star Fatty Arbuckle and his entourage held a wild party and a starlet died. Arbuckle was arrested and later acquitted, but his career was over.

After the 1906 earthquake destroyed their home, George Pope and his wife moved into the hotel and some say they never checked out. Many guests have commented on strange noises and apparitions in these rooms. During WWII high-ranking military personnel held strategic meetings in the Pope Suite named after the erstwhile George Pope.

After the war the St. Francis hosted many of the international delegations that came to San Francisco for the United Nations charter signing. The Russians were the most memorable. The lobby clock was a master clock that kept time for every room in the building. It worked like a charm from 1907 until 1945 when the Russians saw wires in their rooms (connecting to the master clock), assumed they were being bugged, and clipped the cords.

In the 1930s women who came downtown wore white gloves, and, because coins could leave smudges, the hotel polished their change in a silver burnishing machine.

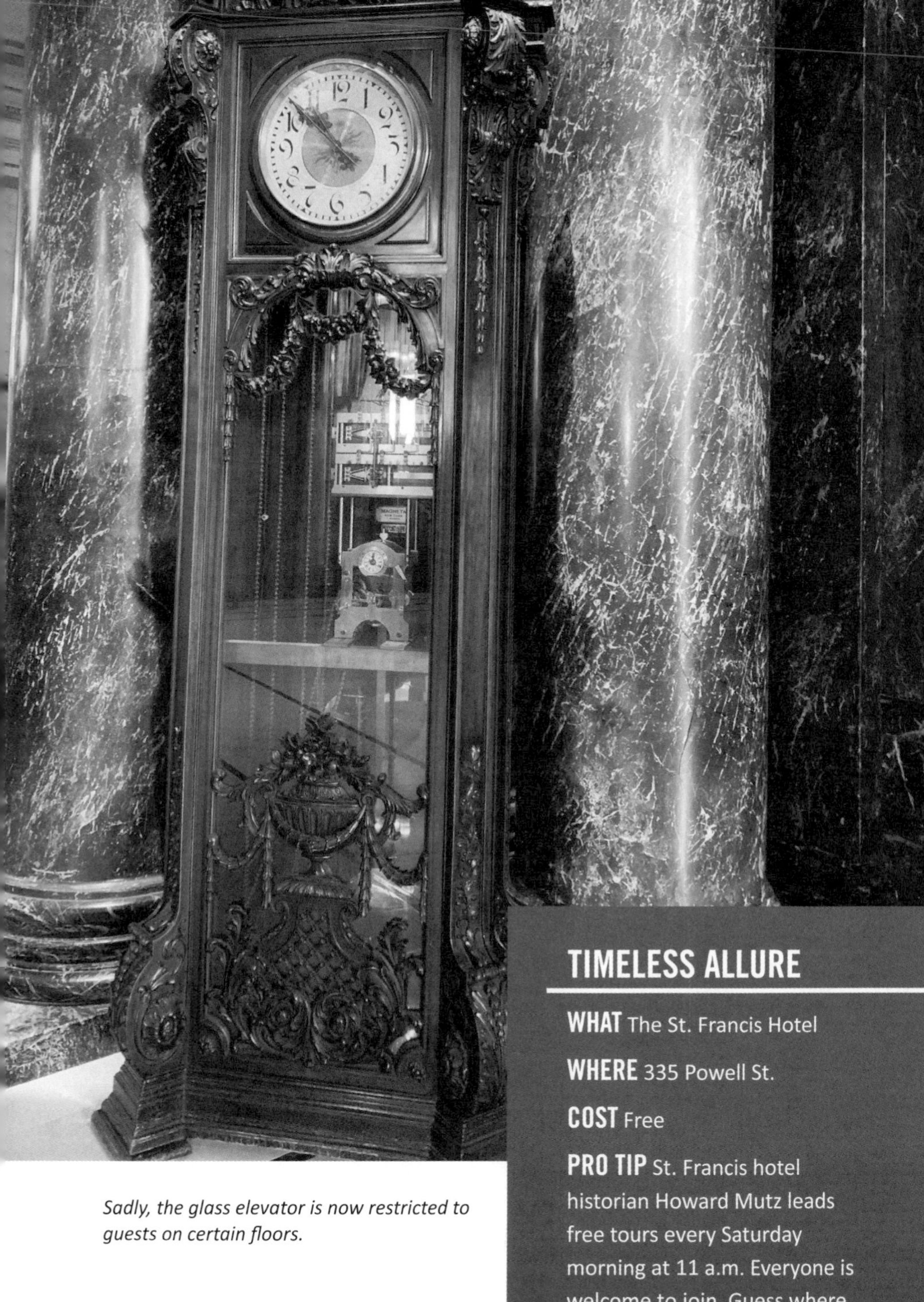

Sadly, the glass elevator is now restricted to guests on certain floors.

TIMELESS ALLURE

WHAT The St. Francis Hotel

WHERE 335 Powell St.

COST Free

PRO TIP St. Francis hotel historian Howard Mutz leads free tours every Saturday morning at 11 a.m. Everyone is welcome to join. Guess where they meet?

82 POWER OF PUBLIC DISCOURSE

What is the Commonwealth Club of California?

In 1903 San Franciscans engaged in an experiment. Reporters, professors, lawyers, and authors concerned about government actions formed a non-partisan group to discuss current events. Views as diverse as possible were welcomed in order that no point of view may be missed, wrote the *San Francisco Chronicle*.

Politicians, who listened to speakers on groundbreaking subjects such as child labor, Native American rights, and air pollution, often took legislative action. In 1924 the Club began broadcasting the talks nationally on the airwaves and now it's the oldest continuing radio show in the country.

The experiment was successful; the Commonwealth Club of California is the nation's first and largest public affairs program.

"We have the largest breadth of public affairs programs available to the public," says spokesperson Riki Rafner. "Our programs are of interest to anyone and everyone," says Rafner. Speakers have included presidents, such as Franklin Roosevelt, and the topics have covered everything from wildfires to climate change.

The Club's mission has not changed but the location has; to a new building across from the Ferry Building—also a great place to see the Blue Angels and New Year's Eve fireworks, according to Rafner.

In 1931 the Commonwealth Club established a Book Award and recipients have included John Steinbeck, William Saroyan, and Amy Tan.

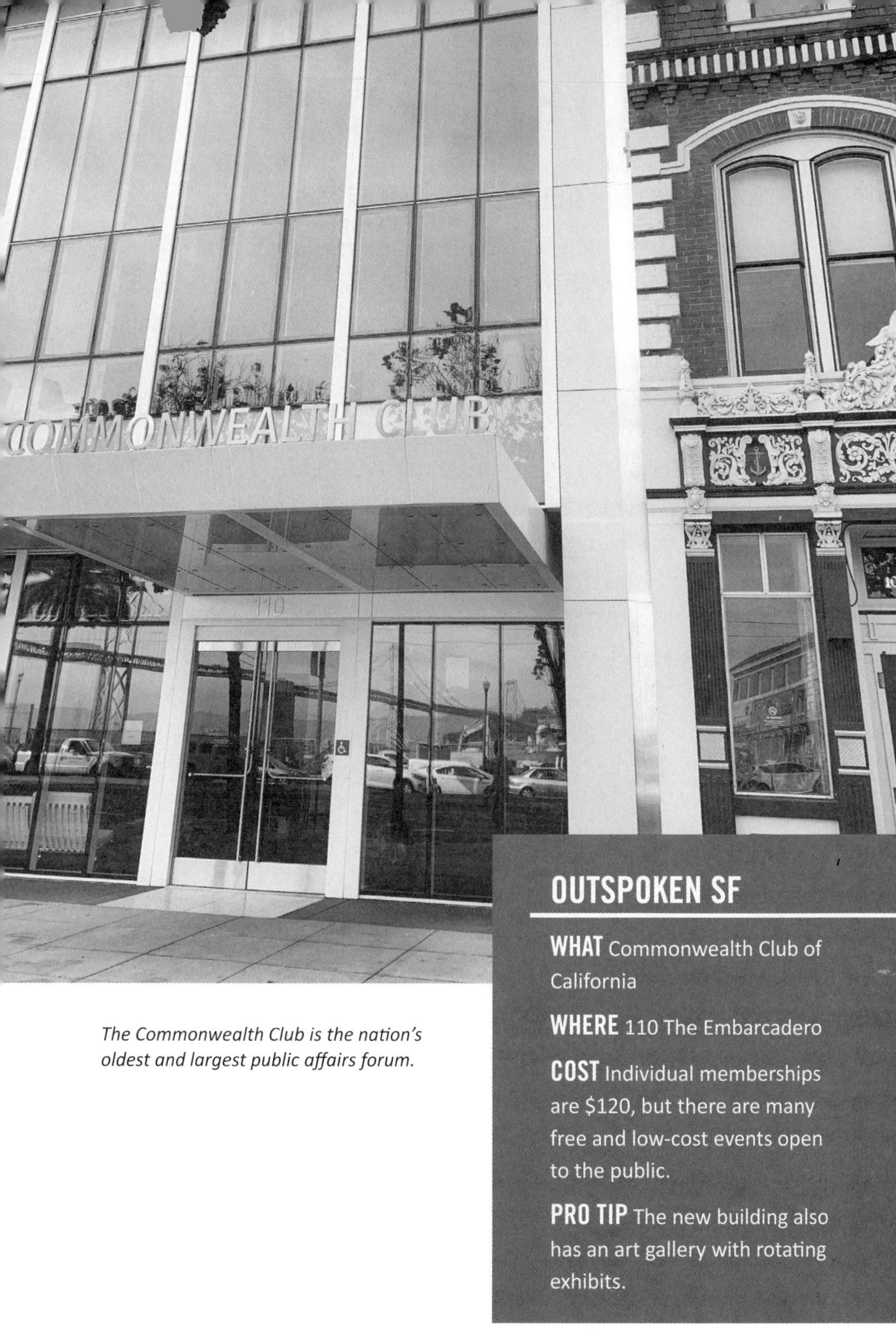

The Commonwealth Club is the nation's oldest and largest public affairs forum.

OUTSPOKEN SF

WHAT Commonwealth Club of California

WHERE 110 The Embarcadero

COST Individual memberships are $120, but there are many free and low-cost events open to the public.

PRO TIP The new building also has an art gallery with rotating exhibits.

83 HYDE THAT RESERVOIR

What is that big hole in the ground?

The Hyde Street cable car is a favorite with tourists, taking them to iconic Lombard Street and Ghirardelli Square. Along the way there are postcard—worthy views of San Francisco, Coit Tower, the Bay Bridge, and Golden Gate—and a big hole in the ground. Wait, what is that ugly huge cavern doing on this picturesque hill?

It's the former Francisco reservoir, now a four-acre pit surrounded by a chain link fence. Since 1940 the future of this space has been controversial. Unbelievably, for "the City that knows how," this eyesore has been here since 1940.

The Public Utilities Commission (PUC) has repeatedly tried to sell the parcel to developers, but residents want to avoid a repeat of the Fontana Towers, condos that block views of Aquatic Park.

In 2006 the neighbors finally triumphed. The Francisco Park Conservancy has raised more than $22 million to build a stunning new green space. The new park will include a children's playground, a fenced dog run, community garden, and viewing terraces.

Currently the Conservancy is raising $25 million to build Francisco Park. You can see the park design at franciscopark.org.

San Francisco is the first city in the nation with every resident living within a ten-minute walk of a park or open space, according to the Trust for Public Land.

Residents are happy the new park will include a dog park.

PARK IT

WHAT Future home of the Francisco Park

WHERE South of Bay between Hyde and Larkin Sts.

COST Free

PRO TIP Natureinthecity.org has maps to all the outdoor public spaces in San Francisco.

84 NATIONAL LANDMARK IN DANGER

Why does the Aquatic Pier need to be saved?

Swimming and water shows were all the rage in the 1930s, and these aquatic activities were aided by a WPA project; building the Aquatic Park Pier that serves as a breakwater. This crescent shaped concrete structure is part of an unusual National Park that includes the Hyde St. Pier historic ships, the Maritime Museum, and swimming cove.

Over the years the pier has suffered structural damage from boat crashes; an Army tug in the 1940s, and a freighter in the 1950s, but the constant pounding waves are the main reason the concrete is slowly disintegrating. If the protective Pier is gone swells could damage the historic schooners, a paddlewheel tug, and a steam ferryboat, in addition to making the cove more treacherous for swimmers.

Walkers, bikers, and fishermen enjoy the view from the Pier daily but when large public events occur, officials close it for fear of collapse. Carol Walker, founder of Save Aquatic Park Pier, says the pier can't be refurbished; it has to be replaced, which will take five years and at least $130 million. If they do

---

The Maritime Museum, originally a bathhouse, recently uncovered WPA murals they have restored.

The Pier serves as a breakwater that protects swimmers and historic ships.

SEA CHANGES

WHAT Aquatic Pier

WHERE Below Ghirardelli Square, to the left of Fisherman's Wharf.

COST Free

PRO TIP You can tour the historic ships at Hyde St. Pier.

rebuild the Pier will be at a higher sea level to account for climate changes.

Walker stepped up to save the Pier because she has fond memories of Aquatic Park. "I always loved the waterfront," she says. "In the fifties there were lots of nighttime activities there. It was quite the party place," she laughs. She hopes the Pier is saved for future generations to enjoy.

85 ON THE MARK

Where can someone in military get a free drink?

As the sun sets over cable cars chugging up Nob Hill, lighting up the Ferry Building clock, it's easy to imagine you're back in the 1940s when soldiers preparing for war toasted to the Golden Gate Bridge for good luck and vowed to meet again at the Top of the Mark. San Francisco was the gateway to the Pacific theater and the Top of the Mark, located on the highest floor of the Intercontinental Mark Hopkins Hotel, had a panoramic view of the ships heading to war. So many wives, sweethearts, and sisters gathered in the lounge to wave goodbye to their men, the section was called "Weepers Corner."

Soldiers on leave headed straight for this swanky location where they could dance to big bands broadcasting live on the radio. One soldier bought a bottle of liquor, signed the label with his squadron's name and asked the bartender to give returning members of his unit access to the hooch. There was one requirement for the free shot, whoever drank the last drop had to buy a new bottle. The idea caught on and soon there were dozens of designated bottles, usually bourbon, behind the bar. Imbibers were asked to write in a journal, a sentimental and unofficial way to keep track of who made it back from the war.

Longtime fans of the Mark will be thrilled to know that the famed circular bar will soon return to its rightful place in the center of the room.

The Intercontinental Mark Hopkins hotel is named after railroad baron Mark Hopkins.

After the war the tradition was lost until 2009 when LT Mike Hall of Pacifica bought a bottle of Wild Turkey and started a new logbook. The bottles and diaries are kept in a locked case next to the host station and opened up whenever a soldier or veteran visits.

TOP OF THE MARK

WHAT Historic penthouse bar

WHERE Top floor of the Intercontinental Mark Hopkins hotel

COST Whatever you choose to spend on appetizers and drinks.

PRO TIP There's a small museum on the first floor of the hotel worth visiting and if you're lucky, the Room of the Dons will be open and you'll see murals depicting early California.

86 RESTORING DOGPATCH

What's one of the fastest growing areas of San Francisco?

Like the serpentine rock it's built on, Dogpatch has a meandering history. It's listed on the National Registry as the Union Iron Works Historic District because it was once among the most productive shipbuilding sites in the world.

Shipyard workers, mostly Irish, needed housing, so local architect John Cotter Pelton Jr. designed "Cheap Dwellings," inexpensive yet stylish Victorian cottages that still exist in the 1000 block of Tennessee St. The newspaper published the plans for free, believed to be the only time a California architect performed this service.

These houses, along with many of the area's industrial structures, survived the 1906 earthquake, and have been preserved. Nearby brick warehouses are undergoing restoration, or if that's not feasible, the storefronts are used as facades for high tech offices, bakeries, restaurants, artists' lofts, and apartments. Developers even kept the large serpentine boulder known as Irish Hill, one of the last remnants of the initial Irish Catholic community.

With the Warriors basketball stadium under construction nearby and a planned walking path linking the area to trails along the city's waterfront, Dogpatch will continue making history.

There are many rumors about the origin of the name Dogpatch. Some say its named after a pack of dogs that used to roam the old meatpacking area while others say its name comes from the *Li'l Abner* comic strip.

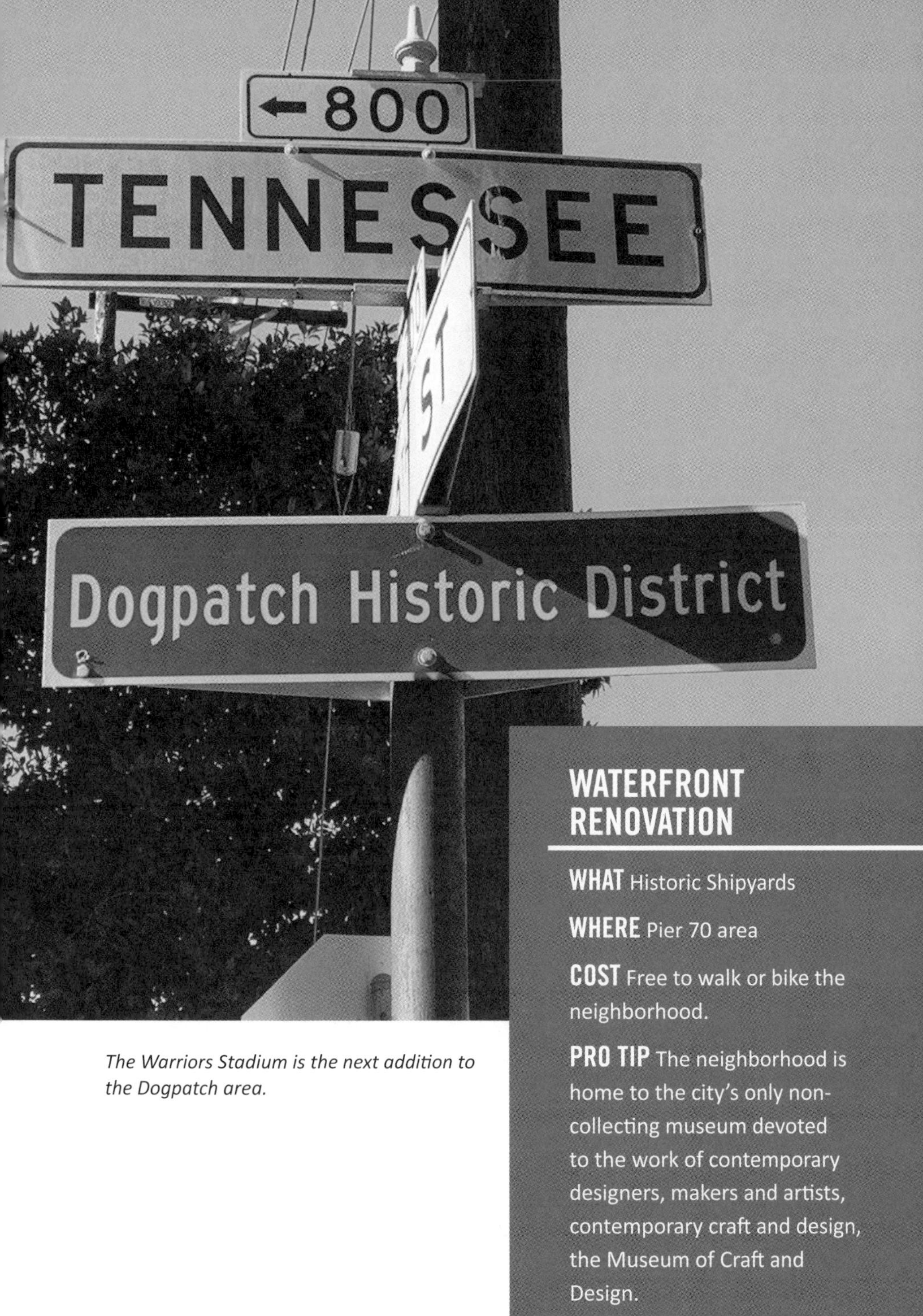

The Warriors Stadium is the next addition to the Dogpatch area.

WATERFRONT RENOVATION

WHAT Historic Shipyards

WHERE Pier 70 area

COST Free to walk or bike the neighborhood.

PRO TIP The neighborhood is home to the city's only non-collecting museum devoted to the work of contemporary designers, makers and artists, contemporary craft and design, the Museum of Craft and Design.

87 FLOWER POWER

Where can you find flowers to wear in your hair?

The ugly warehouses don't look like much from the outside, but when you enter the San Francisco Flower Mart, you're overwhelmed by the colors: pink chrysanthemums, purple hydrangeas, orange birds of paradise, and fiery red gingers. Martha Stewart, the entertainment queen, calls it the best flower market in the country.

"We have the best selection due to our weather, and we're close to the airport so we can bring in fresh flowers from South America, Australia, and Japan," says Jeanne Boes, General Manager. It's also a one-stop shop, where florists can find baskets, vases and ribbons; everything they need for the huge arrangements you see at hotels, restaurants, and special events. Professional florists show up at the crack of dawn, but consumers are not allowed in until 10 a.m.

One of only five flower growers markets in the United States, the San Francisco Mart can trace its origins back to the late 1800s when growers sold bouquets at Lotta's fountain on Market Street. In the early 1900s they started selling indoors.

During WWII when Japanese American growers were sent to internment camps, they continued to hold board meetings, enabling them to start up immediately after the war ended.

Flowers take over the DeYoung Museum for one week each spring during Bouquets to Art. Florists from around the world shop at the Flower Mart to create masterpieces inspired by the museum's artwork.

After work florists dine at Bechelli's Café.

TAKE TIME TO SMELL THE ROSE

WHAT Flower Mart

WHERE 640 Brannan St.

COST Free admission, but you need to ask growers for prices.

PRO TIP Talk to the growers. If they don't have a flower you're looking for, they're happy to refer you to their competition.

Today vendors still do things the old-fashioned way: hand-writing tags, carefully wrapping flowers in old newspaper, negotiating prices, and trimming flowers by request. "It's a piece of old SF," says Boes, who notes the Mart has many legacy businesses run by the same families for generations.

In 2020 the Flower Mart building will be renovated, and the growers will temporarily relocate to a site yet to be determined.

88 SQUEEZE BOX CITY

What is San Francisco's official instrument?

On a tour of Alcatraz you'll see a squeeze box in one of the former inmate's cells, proving the old adage: "play an accordion, go to jail." Despite that dire warning the San Francisco Board of Supervisors bravely passed a resolution making the accordion the city's official musical instrument. It was a successful publicity stunt in 1990 for the band named Those Darn Accordions.

On the day of the vote, band member Tom Torriglia asked his fellow musicians to play accordions on the steps of City Hall. "It was the most ridiculous idea I could think of," says Torriglia, "and the media came out in droves."

The City's proclamation states that the first piano accordion was manufactured in San Francisco in 1907. Originally accordions had buttons until a pianist suggested replacing them with piano keys. This new-fangled instrument was showcased at the 1915 World's Fair. Torriglia says that was "the golden age of accordions" when there were eight businesses producing accordions in the Bay Area, and the world's first accordion club was formed here.

Supervisor Angela Alioto wanted the official instrument to be a violin, in part because her father, the former mayor, played one.

Deborah Wendt is a member of a local band, Diablo Rhythm Wranglers.

Torriglia, now with ladyofspain.com, points out that accordions appear to be having a renaissance with a surprising number of young people interested in learning the instrument. Most musicians head to Smythe's store to purchase their instruments, the only public accordion center in the Bay Area.

DARN ACCORDIONS

WHAT Smythe's, the only public accordion center in the Bay Area.

WHERE Oakland (about thirty minutes away); can be reached by BART, Bay Area Rapid Transit.

COST Free to peruse the accordions. The author cannot be held responsible if you purchase a squeezebox.

PRO TIP Your best bet to hear accordions in the city: North Beach spots such as Caffe Trieste and German beer halls such as Schroeders.

89 THIS IS A TEST

Why does San Francisco still have an air raid siren?

Every Tuesday at noon tourists look up at the sky trying to figure out who's saying, "This is a test, this is only a test." The voice is coming from speakers on poles and rooftops installed during World War II when the city wanted to warn residents of air raids. Today the broadcast is intended to alert people about natural disasters, such as a tsunami.

An actual person in the office of San Francisco Department of Emergency Services turns on the recording that begins with a fifteen-second siren followed by the message, "This is a test. This is a test of the outdoor public warning system. This is only a test." The robotic-sounding voice belongs to Dave Morey, a former radio host with KFOG radio.

If there's a real disaster, the siren will stay on for five minutes and a live voice will tell people what to do.

San Francisco has never had to use the system, but in November 2014 the alert accidentally went off in the middle of the night.

FALSE ALARM

WHAT Outdoor Warning System

WHERE Numerous locations throughout the city.

COST Free

PRO TIP There's a Yelp page reviewing the San Francisco outdoor warning system.

Ham radio operators throughout the city volunteer to listen for the siren and report any glitches.

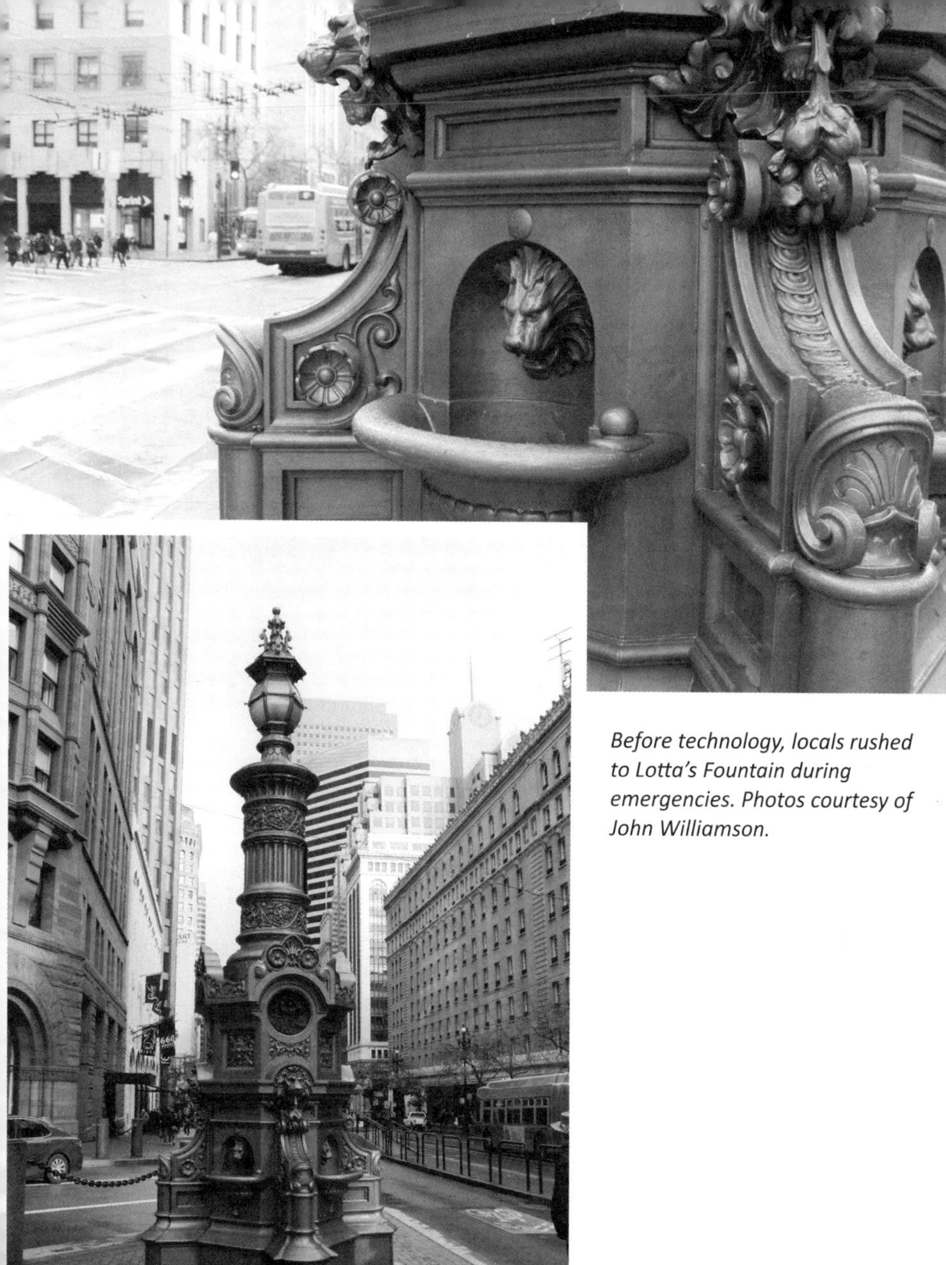

Before technology, locals rushed to Lotta's Fountain during emergencies. Photos courtesy of John Williamson.

90 PARKLETS

Where can I park my derriere?

It's exhausting walking up the hills of San Francisco, but if you can't grab a cable car, don't sweat it—the city has you covered. They've created Parklets, a sliver of land replacing a parking spot. These sidewalk extensions with benches, plants, and often artwork are usually add-ons to cafés' outdoor seating but they're not just for customers—anyone can sit there.

Design firm Rebar created the Pavement to Parks program. When members realized there are no restrictions on what you can do with a parking space, as long as you feed the meter, they rolled out AstroTurf, set down a bench, and converted asphalt into a temporary park.

San Francisco took notice and decided to make parklets permanent. Perhaps they knew that sidewalks used to be wider until cars came along and streets were expanded.

Scattered throughout the city, the designs include: wooden benches with landscaping, modular parklets, colorful umbrellas with a string of lights over high stools, one that resembles a ship sailing down the street, and a modified Citroën cycling van.

The idea has taken off internationally. Every third Friday of September is PARK(ing) Day, where people occupy parking spaces with chairs instead of cars. Some of the more unusual uses: a Ping-Pong tournament in Los Angeles and a huge Pokémon erected on a parklet in Singapore.

Parklets are sponsored by businesses, community organizations or residents.

PARK IT

WHAT Dozens of snippets of land designed for relaxing.

WHERE All over town

COST Free

PRO TIP Many of the parklets include free Wi-Fi and some have vertical bicycle storage.

They've been used for weddings, business meetings, puppet shows, plays, election viewing parties, and brown-bag lunches but primarily for people watching. Businesses, neighborhood groups, schools and museums sponsor these pocket parks.

SOURCES

Al's Attire: Interview with Al Ribaya, www.afar.com/places/als-attire-san-francisco

Art House: Tour and Interview with Gregangelo Herrera, owner, Gregangelo Museum, www.sfchronicle.com/entertainment/article/Modest-looking-city-house-opens-door-to-magical, https://thebolditalic.com/the-crazy-circus-house-in-san-francisco

Book Club Oprah Would Love: Interview with Kevin Kiosk, Executive Director, Book Club of California, www.atlasobscura.com/places/book-club-of-california

Back to the Future: Interview with Thomas Escher, Chairman and CEO, Red and White Fleet, www.mercurynews.com/2018/09/13/first-of-its-kind-hybrid-electric-ferry-boat-to-take-maiden-voyage-in-sf-bay, www.sfchronicle.com/bayarea/article/Bay-Area-to-build-first-hydrogen-fuel-cell-ferry

Bank on It: Interview with Todd Mayberry, Associate Museum Manager, Heritage Marketing and Museums, Wells Fargo Brand Engagement, Interview with Rick Evans, San Francisco Architecture Tour, www.architecturesf.com,www.artandarchitecture-sf.com/the-first-national-bank-building.html

Bars with a Story Part I: Site visits and interviews with regulars and bartenders, *Drinking the Devil's Acre, A Love Letter from San Francisco and her Cocktails*, by Duggan McDonnell, *High Spirits: The Legacy Bars of San Francisco* by J.K. Dineen, www.atlasobscura.com/places/the-old-ship-saloon, www.sf.curbed.com/2016/11/14/13625698/old-ship-saloon-excavated-san-francisco,www.sftravel.com/article/oldest-bars-san-francisco-neighborhood, https://theculturetrip.com/north-america/usa/california/articles/the-saloon-the-oldest-bar-in-sf-is-your-new-go-to-spot

Bars with a Story Part II: Interviews Shanti Deluca, Bartender, House of Shields and James King, owner, Black Horse London Pub, *High Spirits: The Legacy Bars of San Francisco* by J.K. Dineen, *Drinking the Devil's Acre, A Love Letter from San Francisco and her Cocktails*, by Duggan McDonnell, www.travelandleisure.com/articles/san-francisco-best-dive-bars

Beat Goes On: Interview Janet Clyde, co-owner, Vesuvio, Tour of Beat Museum, www.washingtonpost.com 2017 the-beat-generation, https://savingplaces.org/stories/historic-bars-san-franciscos-vesuvio-cafe, www.sftravel.com/take-beat-era-north-beach-walking-tour

Best Place to Get Lost: Site Visit, Interviews Creator Edward Aguilera and Keeper Colleen Yerge www.smithsonianmag.com/travel/walk-worlds-meditative-labyrinths, www.atlasobscura.com/places/labyrinth-lands-end, https://www.sfchronicle.com/bayarea/cityexposed/article/Lands-End-labyrinth-keeper

Burning Man: Interview with John Law, one of the founders, Tales of the San Francisco Cacophony Society by Carrie Galbraith and John Law, https://newrepublic.com/article/150497/vanishing-idealism-burning-man, www.outsideonline.com/1925281/hot-mess

Camera Obscura: Site Visit, www.atlasobscura.com/places/camera-obscura-holograph, www.sfchronicle.com/thetake/article/The-Regulars-Camera-Obscura-still-makes-a-big

Camera Ready: Site Visit, Interview Allie Haeusslein, Assoc. Dir., Pier 24 Photography, www.newyorker.com/culture/photo-booth/on-and-off-the-walls-a-first-look-at-pier-24

Checkmate: Tour and interview Bobbie Monzon, Director of Operations, Mechanics Institute, www.sfcityguides.org, www.kqed.org/arts/76913/the_mechanics_institute_an_historical_oasis,www.atlasobscura.com/places/mechanics-institute-library-and-chess-room

Christmas Con: Interview with John Law, one of the founders of SF SantaCon, www.sfchronicle.com/bayarea/article/SantaCon-in-San-Francisco-Ready-or-not, www.kqed.org/news/11707402/how-santacon-got-its-start-in-san-francisco-counterculture, www.atlasobscura.com/articles/the-danish-anarchists-who-inspired-santacon-could-not-have-imagined-its-brohell-future, www.atlasobscura.com/articles/the-danish-anarchists-who-inspired-santacon-could-not-have-imagined-its-brohell-future

Cheesy Education: Interview with owner Kiri Fisher, instructor Laura Werlin, www.sftravel.com/explore/cheese-school-san-francisco, https://blog.sfgate.com/culture/2011/05/23/tourist-trapped-the-cheese-school-of-san-francisco, https://www.sfchronicle.com/entertainment/article/The-cheese-definitely-does-not-stand-alone

City Paved with Gravestones: www.sfchronicle.com/bayarea/article/How-San-Francisco-evicted-thousands-of-dead-people, www.exploratorium.edu/visit/wave-organ, www.atlasobscura.com/places/wave-organ, www.atlasobscura.com/places/buena-vista-park-tombstones

City Guides: Interview Jef Friedel, Program Manager, SF City Guides, http://www.sfcityguides.org,www.sfgate.com/bayarea/article/Gladys-Hansen-SF-archivist-and-1906-earthquake

Costly Cable Cars: Visit to Cable Car Museum, www.sfchronicle.com/bayarea/article/The-year-the-cable-car-haters-almost-ruined, https://sf.curbed.com/2017/9/20/16338488/cable-cars-facts-sf, www.sfchronicle.com/oursf/article/All-Down-the-Line-When-Mick-Jagger-pitched-in

Creativity Explored: Site visit, Interviews Executive Director, Linda Johnson, Studio Director Paul Moshammer, www.sfchronicle.com/entertainment/article/Monsters-as-art-form-at-Creativity-Explored, *100 Things to Do in San Francisco Before you Die* by Eve Batey and Patricia Corrigan

Critical Mass: Interview Chris Carlsson, one of the founders of San Francisco Critical Mass, *San Francisco, the Unknown City* by Helene Goupil and Josh Krist, *Shift Happens! Critical Mass at 20* Edited by Chris Carlsson, LisaRuth Elliott, and Adriana Camarena, www.sfchronicle.com/bayarea/nevius/article/Critical-Mass-is-dying-of-self-inflicted-wounds, www.foundsf.org/index.php?title=Category:Bicycling

Dog Heaven: Interview Amanda Williford, curator, Presidio Park Archives and Records,

www.atlasobscura.com/places/san-franciscos-pet-cemetery

Doggie Diner: Interview John Law, owner of three Doggie Diner heads, DoggieDiner.com, https://www.roadsideamerica.com/story/14441, http://www.foundsf.org/index.php?title=Doggie_Diner

Dutch Treat: https://goldengatepark.com/windmills.html, www.nytimes.com/2010/07/11/us/11bcintel.html, https://hoodline.com/2017/03/getting-to-know-golden-gate-park-s-elusive-windmills, www.atlasobscura.com/places/murphy-windmill, www.sfchronicle.com/chronicle_vault/article/The-Golden-Gate-Park-windmills-are-survivors

Earthquake Shacks: Visited shacks on the Presidio, Interview Joe Butler, Architect and SF Historian, https://sf.curbed.com/2015/2/24/9988502/remembering-earthquake-shacks-san-franciscos-original-tiny-houses, www.nps.gov/prsf/learn/historyculture/1906-earthquake-relief-efforts-living-accommodations.htm

Emperor with No Clothes: Tour and Interview with Joseph Amster, Emperor Norton's Fantastic Time Machine, www.sfmuseum.org/hist1/norton.html,www.foundsf.org/index.php?title=Emperor_Norton

Escape from the Concrete: Site Visits, Architecture Tour Rick Evans, https://sf.curbed.com/maps/sf-parks-private-popos-public-owned https://sfpopos.com, www.spur.org/sites/default/files/migrated/anchors/popos-guide.pdf, www.daily.co/blog/top-sf-public-private-spaces-3-best-places-to-work, https://thebolditalic.com/an-illustrated-guide-to-finding-sfs-privately-owned-public-spaces

First Skyscraper: Architecture Tour with Rick Evans, https://sf.curbed.com/2018/3/7/17073432/hallidie-building-glass-curtain-history-san-francisco, www.aiasf.org/page/25Buildings

Fishy Tale: Interview Nancy Uber Rose, spokesperson, Scomas, www.sftravel.com/article/definitive-history-cioppino-san-francisco, www.kqed.org/news/11695791/the-fishy-origins-of-cioppino, www.montereyherald.com/2009/01/28/chip-in-o-the-colorful-history-of-cioppino, https://avitaltours.com/san-francisco/history-of-san-francisco-cioppino

Foggy Friend: Mike Pechner, meteorologist, www.tripsavvy.com/san-francisco-fog-viewing, www.sftravel.com/article/fun-facts-about-san-francisco-fog,www.sfchronicle.com/news/article/How-Karl-the-Fog-rolls-Twitter-presence

Float in North Beach: Attended several festivals, www.usatoday.com/story/travel/2018/10/04/san-franciscos-north-beach-celebrates-150-years-italian-heritage, www.sfchronicle.com/oursf/article/Our-city-For-150-years-San-Francisco-has-loved

Flower Power: Site Visits, Interview Jeanne Boes, General Manager, www.newyorker.com/business/currency/flower-struggle, www.sftravel.com/article/springtime-blooms-san-francisco

Flying Boats: Site visits Treasure Island, Oakland Aviation Museum, www.panam.org/war-years/400-how-america-s-airline-went-to-war-2, www.artandarchitecture-sf.com/san-franciscos-first-airport.html, www.treasureislandmuseum.org/island-history

French Connection: Interview Gilles Lorand, www.sanfranciscobygilles.com, https://noehill.com/sf/landmarks/nat1975000471.asp, www.foundsf.org/index.php?title=The_City_of_Paris

Free Trip Around the World: Shanghaied in San Francisco by Bill Pickelhaupt, Site visit Maritime Museum, www.atlasobscura.com/places/site-of-the-san-francisco-hippodrome, www.foundsf.org/index.php?title=Shanghaiing, www.sfcityguides.org/public_guidelines.html

Ghostly Landmark: Site Visit and Tour, www.atlasobscura.com/places/san-francisco-columbarium,www.sfchronicle.com/thetake/article/Life-within-the-San-Francisco-Columbarium

Historic Hijinks: Interview Robert J. Chandler, author An E Clampus Vitus Hoax Goes Awry, www.sfgate.com/food/article/Toastin-and-plaquin-California-s-drinkin-, www.nytimes.com/2008/10/14/us/14california.html

Historic Wins: Interview Renel Brooks-Moon, public address announcer, SF Giants, Shana Daum, Vice President of Public Affairs & Community Relations, San Francisco Giants, www.huffingtonpost.com/2014/07/28/renel-brooks-moon, www.mercurynews.com/2011/06/03/renel-brooks-moon-scores-with-fans-at-the-ballpark-and-on-the-radio/

Hotel of International Intrigue: Interview and tour of St. Francis with hotel historian Howard Mutz, www.foundsf.org/index.php?title=The_Weird_History of_the_St._Francis_Hotel, www.atlasobscura.com/places/westin-st-francis-hotel, www.bbc.com/news/magazine-14640719

Hotel with a Heart: Interview, Community Projects Manager, Jo Licata, www.sfchronicle.com/thetake/article/Beatles-in-SF-Treasure-trove-of-photos-found-50-9111252.php

How the Bay was Saved: Site Visit San Francisco Bay-Delta Model, https://boomcalifornia.com/2015/04/14/the-man-who-helped-save-san-francisco-bay-by-trying-to-destroy-it, www.atlasobscura.com/places/bay-model, www.sfchronicle.com/thetake/article/How-a-giant-model-of-SF-Bay-helped-science

Human Lie Detector: Interview with Jay Alexander, www.sfgate.com/performance/article/Underneath-Moroccan-restaurant-magic-show

Hyde That Reservoir: Site visit, Interview Emily Harrold, volunteer public relations, Francisco Park, https://nobhillgazette.com/local-park-boosters-eye-the-finish-line, www.franciscopark.org/history, www.sfchronicle.com/bayarea/article/Russian-Hill-park-expected-on-abandoned-reservoir, www.foundsf.org/index.php?title=Francisco_Reservoir

Imposter: sf.funcheap.com, sf.funcheap.com, www.sfcityguides.org, www.mercurynews.com/2015/12/08/the-most-crooked-street-in-san-francisco, http://bringyourownbigwheel.com/

Inside Alcatraz: Interview Jolene Babyak, former resident and warden's daughter, www.history.com/news/10-things-you-may-not-know-about-alcatraz, www.thetravel.com/surprising-things-about-alcatraz-only-the-guards-knew/

It's a Wonderful Life: Interviews, Tom Escher, CEO & Chairman, Red and White Fleet, David Mendoza, Bank of America historian, www.pbs.org/wgbh/theymadeamerica/whomade/giannini_hi.html,www.mercurynews.com/2017/10/04/matters-historical-how-a-clever-young-italian-american-created-a-powerful-bank, www.todayifoundout.com/index.php/2011/06/the-real-life-george-bailey-who-founded-bank-of-italy-which-became-bank-of-america/, www.sfchronicle.com/oursf/article/Our-SF-A-P-Giannini-a-banker

Lawn Bowling: Site Visit and interviews with members John Grimes and Daniel Gorelick, www.atlasobscura.com/places/golden-gate-park-lawn-bowling-club, www.sfgate.com/bayarea/article/S-F-lawn-bowlers-share-their-time-tested-sport

Leaning Tower of San Francisco: Rick Evans, Architecture Walking Tour, www.businessinsider.com/is-millennium-tower-safe-still-leaning-sinking, www.sfgate.com/bayarea/article/Millennium-Tower-keeps-on-sinking

Leaving a Legacy: Interview Mike Buhler, president of SF Heritage Society, *High Spirits, The Legacy Bars of San Francisco*, www.bizjournals.com/sanfrancisco/news/2017/08/17/legacy-business-program-sf-works-retail-government.html, www.sfchronicle.com/bayarea/article/San-Francisco-approves-first-nine-legacy

Mainland Hawaii: Interviews with Uke Club members, Margery Moran, Andy Andrews, site visits, www.santacruz.org/blog/article/106/uke-ing-in-santa-cruz, www.santacruzsentinel.com/2009/04/23/the-ukulele-club-of-santa-cruz-has-turned-a-once-laughed-at-musical-instrument-into-a-tool-to-build-community

Meow for the Masses: Site visit, www.sfchronicle.com/entertainment/article/A-trip-to-S-F-s-KitTea-cat-cafe, https://sf.curbed.com/2015/6/19/9948136/first-look-inside-the-kittea-cat-cafe-as-it-gears-up-for-opening

Model Club: Site visit to Model Yacht Club and interview with Vice Commodore Rob Weaver

www.sfchronicle.com/bayarea/article/Tradition-of-model-boats-a-treasure

Mr. San Francisco: Baghdad by the Bay by Herb Caen, The World of Herb Caen, edited by Barnaby Conrad, www.sfchronicle.com/bayarea/heatherknight/article/Herb-Caen-lives-on-via-Twitter-and-a-faraway. www.sfchronicle.com/bayarea/place/article/Problems-Herb-Caen-saw-in-1948-San-Francisco-6171450.php, www.nytimes.com/1997/02/02/us/herb-caen-80-san-francisco-voice-dies.html

Murals with a Message: Site visit. Interview with Patricia Rose, Precita Eyes Muralists, https://sf.curbed.com/maps/49-of-san-franciscos-most-awesome-murals-mapped, www.sftravel.com/article/guide-san-francisco-mission-district-murals

National Landmark in Danger: Site visit, interview Carol Walker, founder of Save Aquatic Park Pier,

www.sfchronicle.com/bayarea/nativeson/article/Municipal-Pier-crumbling-but-no-money-to-rebuild,

www.sfgate.com/bayarea/article/Iconic-Municipal-Pier-at-Aquatic-Park-pier

Nature Friends: Interview. jay Gustafson, member The Nature Friends Tourist Club https://touristclubsf.org/

Nothing to Hide: www.kqed.org/news/11613510/the-history-of-nudity-in-san-francisco-uncovered,

www.nytimes.com/2012/11/21/us/san-francisco-officials-vote-to-ban-public-nudity.html, www.sfchronicle.com/bayarea/article/S-F-barely-passes-public-nudity-ban

Ocean Liner House: Site Visit, https://sf.curbed.com/2016/4/8/11395718/art-deco-condo-telegraph-hill-dark-passage-malloch-building, www.sfgate.com/bayarea/article/Malloch-building-suave-delight-on-storied-hill-3295785.php, www.artandarchitecture-sf.com/1360-montgomery-street-streamline-moderne-dream.html

On the Mark: Site Visit, Interview with Keelin Marcoux, spokesperson, Mark Hopkins Hotel, www.bostonglobe.com/lifestyle/travel/2015/10/09/high-watering-hole-and-its-place-history, www.ocregister.com/2009/05/22/well-meet-again-at-the-top-of-the-mark, www.theworldofdeej.com/2012/08/top-of-the-mark-san-francisco.html

Page Turner: Site Visit and Tour, www.sfchronicle.com/books/article/Arion-Press-takes-a-page-from-the-past,111 Places in San Francisco That You Must Not Miss, by Fiona Peterson

Parklets: Site visits, https://sf.curbed.com/maps/mapping-all-43-awesome-san-francisco-public-parklets, www.sfpublicworks.org/services/permits/parklets

Peephole Cinema: Site visit, interview with Laurie O'Brien, Peephole Cinema Founder www.atlasobscura.com/places/peephole-cinema, www.flysfo.com/museum/public-art-collection

Phantom Fleet: Visit to Maritime Museum and J. Porter Shaw Library at Fort Mason, https://news.nationalgeographic.com/2017/05/map-ships-buried-san-francisco, https://www.nps.gov/safr/learn/historyculture/buried-ships-in-san-francisco.htm, www.kqed.org/news/11633087/the-buried-ships-of-san-francisco

Pliney Phenomenon: Site Visit, Interviews Spencer Paul General Manager, Russian River Brewing Company and Chris Vomvolakis, Director of Marketing, VisitSantaRosa.com, www.sonomamag.com/pliny-the-younger-release, www.sacbee.com/food-drink/beer/article200194954.html

Power of Public Discourse: Site Visit, interview Riki Rafner, spokesperson Commonwealth Club www.commonwealthclub.org/about/history, www.huffingtonpost.com/2013/01/08/commonwealth-club,https://archpaper.com/2018/08/commonwealth-club-san-francisco-headquarters-honors-union-history,www.sfgate.com/bayarea/article/Commonwealth-Club-moves-into-new-home

Restoring Dogpatch: Site Visit and City Guides Tour, https://sf.curbed.com/2018/1/9/16865788/guide-about-dogpatch-san-francisco-neighborhood,www.sfchronicle.com/bayarea/article/Dogpatch-SF-s-latest-boomtown-neighborhood

Rivera Effect: Site Visits and Tours of murals, www.foundsf.org/index.php?title=Diego_Rivera_in_San_Francisco, https://theculturetrip.com/north-america/usa/california/articles/a-brief-overview-of-diego-riveras-murals-in-san-francisco, www.nytimes.com/1986/06/24/opinion/l-a-reminder-that-diego-rivera-left-his-art-in-san-francisco

Royal Accommodations: Site Visits, Interview Renee Roberts, spokesperson, Palace Hotel, https://sf.curbed.com/2014/3/24/10127954/a-history-of-the-palace-san-franciscos-oldest-surviving-hotel

www.historichotels.org/hotels-resorts/palace-hotel, www.sfchronicle.com/bayarea/nativeson/article/Cleaning-time-at-Palace-Hotel-s-glassy-classy, www.sfgate.com/news/article/S-F-s-new-Palace-Hotel-celebrates-a-century

San Francisco Sendoff: Site Visit, Interviews, Bob Yount, Manager, Green Street Mortuary, Lisa Pollard, Leader, Green St. Mortuary Band, www.youtube.com/watch?v=akY3OBkNtTk, https://www.mercurynews.com/2010/03/17/san-francisco-chinatown-where-the-band-plays-on, https://www.sfgate.com/news/article/HOW-SWEET-THE-SOUND-With-trumpets-and-2963643.php

Sea Squatters: Site Visits, Interview Sheila Chandor, Director, Marina Operations, Pier 39, San Francisco Chronicle archive articles, https://www.sfgate.com/bayarea/article/Famed-sea-lions-vanish-from-Fisherman-s-Wharf-5585563.phphttps://www.pier39.com/the-sea-lion-story/

Seadog Chapel: Site visits, www.artandarchitecture-sf.com/fishermens-and-seamens-chapel.html, www.sfgate.com/bayarea/article/Simple-wood-chapel-defies-Fisherman-s-Wharf-kitsch https://fishermanswharf.org/about/memorial-chapel/

Secret Garden: Site visit, interviews with gardeners, www.fortmasoncommunitygarden.org, https://theculturetrip.com/north-america/usa/california/articles/the-coolest-community-gardens-in-san-francisco/

SF's Good Fortune: Site visit, http://americanhistory.si.edu/blog/2010/07/origins-of-a-fortune-cookie.html, www.discovernikkei.org/en, www.nytimes.com/2008/01/16/travel/16iht-fortune.9260526.html, http://articles.latimes.com/2008/jun/08/local/me-then

Shaking up San Francisco: www.sfchronicle.com/chronicle_vault/article/An-ode-to-the-Embarcadero-Freeway-the-blight-by-teh bay, www.sfgate.com/bayarea/place/article/15-seconds-that-changed-San-Francisco

Shell Game: Architecture tour with Rick Evans, https://sf.curbed.com/2017/11/9/16577156/heineman-building-130-bush-skinny-thin-high-rise, https://noehill.com/sf/landmarks/sf183.asp, https://untappedcities.com/2011/12/09/architecture-spotlight-one-bush-plaza-a-place-of-international-style/,www.loc.gov/item/2013630233

Shootout over Slavery: www.nps.gov/goga/learn/historyculture/broderick-terry-duel.htm, www.foundsf.org/index.php?title=The_Duelwww.atlasobscura.com/places/broderick-terry-duel-site, www.mercurynews.com/2011/10/25/last-duel-in-san-francisco-history-helped-sway-california-to-the-side-of-the-union/

Slowing Down Time: www.artandarchitecture-sf.com/tag/ingleside-terrace-sundial, www.outsidelands.org/sd3.php

Sounds of San Francisco: Attended concert, Interviewed Dave Shaff, Composer/Theater Manager, www.thedailybeast.com/step-inside-audium-san-franciscos-trippy-music-sculpture, www.atlasobscura.com/places/audium-theatre-of-sound

Strange Saga of SF's Song: www.kalw.org/post/san-francisco-s-two-official-songs-or-day-tony-bennett-hid-his-hotel#stream, https://blog.sfgate.com/thebigevent/2012/02/14/not-everyone-loves-i-left-my-heart, http://articles.latimes.com/2012/feb/14/local/la-me-tony-bennett-valentine-20120214

Stairways to Heaven: Site visits, Stairway Walks in San Francisco by Mary Burk, www.sfgate.com/outdoors/article/The-Bay-Area-s-best-staircases-3819256.php, https://sf.curbed.com/building/4432/golden-gate-heights-mosaic-stairway,

Stinky Saturdays: Tour and interview with Beatriz Flórez Huertas, Public Information Officer, San Francisco Public Utilities Commission, www.sfchronicle.com/entertainment/article/Waste-time-in-SF-on-the-great-sewer-tour

Squeezebox City: Interview Tom Torriglia, www.apnews.com/376dd5a7b608f64b18abf834aaafc0fd, www.sfgate.com/entertainment/article/The-Accordion-San-Francisco-s-Official, www.washingtonpost.com/archive/lifestyle/1990/01/09/accordions-the-heart-of-frisco/

Tap It: Interview Suzanne Gautier Manager, Communications, San Francisco Public Utilities Commission, www.sfgate.com/bayarea/article/S-F-to-sell-bottled-Hetch-Hetchy-water-Sierra-2663445.php, www.sfchronicle.com/science/article/SF-Mayor-Breed-vetoes-supes-resolution

Techies Take a Time Out: Site Visit, Interview spokesperson Michael McElligott www.sfchronicle.com/food/article/Long-Now-Foundation-opens-the-Interval-cafe-bar https://sanfrancisco.cbslocal.com/2014/06/15/salon-long-term-thinking-drinks-conversation-opens-fort-mason-center/

This is a Test: www.kqed.org/news/11696396/this-is-only-a-test-san-franciscos-tuesday-noon-siren https://sfdem.org/tuesday-noon-siren www.sfgate.com/bayarea/article/What-is-that-San-Francisco-noon-siren

Tin How Temple: Site visit, 111 Places in San Francisco That You Must Not Miss by Floriana Petersen, San Francisco's Chinatown by Judy Young, www.lonelyplanet.com/usa/san-francisco/attractions/tin-how-temple

Twain's Tumultuous Times: Interview Benjamin Griffin Associate Editor, Mark Twain Project, The Bancroft Library, University of California, Berkeley, Site Visit Cliff House, http://museumca.org/story/mark-twains-trips-cliff-house, www.twainquotes.com/18640625.html, www.sfchronicle.com/bayarea/article/How-Mark-Twain-got-fired-in-San-Francisco, www.foundsf.org/index.php?title=MARK_TWAIN

Urban Jungle: Interview Deb Campbell, spokesperson, SF animal control, www.sfgate.com/bayarea/article/san-francisco-mountain-lion-sighting-marc-benioff, www.sfgate.com/bayarea/article/It-s-that-time-of-year-again-Coyotes, www.sfchronicle.com/bayarea/article/No-matter-how-many-pets-they-kill-SF-s-coyotes

Waterworks: Interviewed Suzanne Gautier, Manager, Communications, San Francisco Public Utilities Commission, www.kqed.org/news/11622273/what-are-the-mysterious-brick-circles-in-san-francisco-intersections, https://untappedcities.com/2012/06/29/cisterns, www.atlasobscura.com/places/1908-cistern-circles, https://sf-fire.org/water-supply-systems

Woman Ahead of Her Time: Site visit, https://sf.curbed.com/2016/9/22/13017182/san-francisco-mary-pleasant-small-park, www.sfcityguides.org/public_guidelines.html?article=1305&submitted=TRUE&srch_text=&submitted2=&topic=, http://newfillmore.com/fillmore-classics/dont-call-her-mammy, www.sfmuseum.org/hist10/mammy.html

When Blue Collars Beat Blue Bloods: Covered the America's Cup races in Spain and San Francisco, The Billionaire and the Mechanic by Julian Guthrie, https://www.nytimes.com/2013/09/05/sports/among-many-differences-americas-cup-is-biggest.html

Whodunnit: Tour with Don Herron, The Dashiell Hammett Tour by Don Herron with preface by Jo Hammett, www.nytimes.com/2014/06/29/travel/san-francisco-noir.html, www.sfgate.com/magazine/

INDEX